COURTNEY *Putnam*

BODY
Cards

INSIGHT FROM THE BODY
Wisdom for the Soul

4880 Lower Valley Road • Atglen, PA 19310

Copyright © 2016 by **COURTNEY PUTNAM**

Library of Congress Control Number: 2016935785

All rights reserved. No part of this work may be reproduced or used in any form or by any means—graphic, electronic, or mechanical, including photocopying or information storage and retrieval systems—without written permission from the publisher.

The scanning, uploading, and distribution of this book or any part thereof via the Internet or any other means without the permission of the publisher is illegal and punishable by law. Please purchase only authorized editions and do not participate in or encourage the electronic piracy of copyrighted materials.

"Schiffer," "Schiffer Publishing, Ltd.," and the pen and inkwell logo are registered trademarks of Schiffer Publishing, Ltd.

Designed by **DANIELLE D. FARMER**
Type set in Telegrafico/Amazone BT/Benton Sans

ISBN: 978-0-7643-5061-0
Printed in China

Published by Schiffer Publishing, Ltd.
4880 Lower Valley Road
Atglen, PA 19310
Phone: (610) 593-1777; Fax: (610) 593-2002
E-mail: Info@schifferbooks.com
Web: www.schifferbooks.com

For our complete selection of fine books on this and related subjects, please visit our website at www.schifferbooks.com. You may also write for a free catalog.

Schiffer Publishing's titles are available at special discounts for bulk purchases for sales promotions or premiums. Special editions, including personalized covers, corporate imprints, and excerpts, can be created in large quantities for special needs. For more information, contact the publisher.

We are always looking for people to write books on new and related subjects. If you have an idea for a book, please contact us at proposals@schifferbooks.com.

Polaroid is a registered trademark of Polaroid Corporation

Brain Gym is a registered trademark of Brain Gym International

Band-Aid is a registered trademark of Johnson & Johnson

Other Schiffer Books on Related Subjects:

Illuminara Intuitive Journal with Cards. Elaine Clayton. ISBN: 978-0-7643-3750-5

Inspiring Butterflies: A 27-Day Course of Self Discovery. Marge Richards and Ginny Zaboronek. ISBN: 978-0-7643-3969-1

Living a Life in Balance: An Elemental Journey of Self-Discovery. Cael SpiritHawk. ISBN: 978-0-7643-4748-1

DEDICATION

FOR ZELDA, WHO TAUGHT ME HOW TO FLY,
FOR MY FATHER, WHO HAS WINGS.

ACKNOWLEDGMENTS

I wish to thank my editor Dinah Roseberry for believing in my vision and embracing both my writing and my art for this project; my writing partner, Kristen Bergsman, for her love, friendship, and creative support; my powerful and compassionate writing group of Ann Teplick, Corbin Lewars, and Teresa Williams; Walter Hudsick and Robyn Ferret, for their invaluable editing help and undying moral support; Natasa Kesler, for her anatomy and physiology expertise; my mom, Ann Putnam, for having a room of her own in which to write and showing me how to inhabit my own; Bev Conner, for her creative support and her generosity of spirit; Binky Bergsman, for mentoring me in encaustic and mixed media art; Ella Nacht, my craniosacral therapist, for allowing me to tap into my body's wisdom in profound ways; my cat, Selkie, for his constant companionship and acceptance; and my husband, Walter, for his fierce love and grounding support.

I also wish to thank every bodywork client I've ever had. It has been an honor to be your guide and witness.

*Your body
is your map your
muse and your medicine*

CONTENTS

INTRODUCTION

Why the Body? 8
Wisdom from the Body 8
About the Chakras 9
About the Art 10

HOW TO USE THE BODY CARDS

Relating to the Cards 11
Selecting the Cards 11
Card Readings 12
Interpreting the Cards 15

THE BODY CARDS

AMYGDALA: Peace 16
ARRECTOR PILI MUSCLES: Retreat 18
CALCANEUS: Foundation 20
CENTRAL NERVOUS SYSTEM:
  Interconnection 22
CEREBELLUM: Grace 24
CEREBRUM: Balance 26
CORNEA: Clarity 28
CORPUS CALLOSUM:
  Communication 30
DIAPHRAGM: Joy 32
FINGERS: Self-assurance 34
GLUTEUS MAXIMUS: Power 36

HEART: Influence 38
KIDNEYS: Priority 40
LARYNX: Expression 42
LIVER: Regeneration 44
MASSETER: Release 46
OLFACTORY BULB: Sensitivity 48
PANCREAS: Authenticity 50
PATELLA: Stability 52
PINEAL GLAND: Intuition 54
PITUITARY GLAND: Delegation 56
QUADRICEPS: Stamina 58
SACRUM: Rebirth 60
SCALENE MUSCLES: Honesty 62
SKIN: Renewal 64
SMALL INTESTINE: Patience 66
SOLEUS MUSCLES: Action 68
SPLEEN: Willpower 70
STERNUM: Protection 72
STIRRUP BONE: Listening 74
STOMACH: Affirmation 76
TEETH: Commitment 78
THYROID GLAND: Transformation 80
UMBILICUS: Connection 82
UTERUS: Manifestation 84

BIBLIOGRAPHY 87

LIST OF CARDS BY CHAKRA 89

INTRODUCTION

Why the Body

We hold deep wisdom in our bodies—in every muscle, bone, blood vessel, nerve fiber, and cell. As John Lee of *Writing from the Body* writes, "Our body holds everything we have ever experienced in our lives, and it remembers." *Body Cards* draws upon the idea that the human body is not only a complex organism complete with the powerful ability to heal, but also a tremendous resource for us in terms of understanding our very lives.

In my career as a massage therapist and Reiki Master, I experienced firsthand how each part of the body has the potential to guide us in understanding ourselves in a deep and meaningful way. Not only does the body "speak" to us in the form of muscle aches, joint pain, and physical illness, but it also has much to say regarding our emotional and psychological life, our stress level, and our overall well being. The potential for growth, transformation, and healing is great when we are able to listen to the messages our body gives us.

Wisdom from the Body

While working with one of my bodywork clients several years ago, I was struck by the power of the human body to "speak" to us. My client was suffering from plantar fasciitis in her right foot, and she came to me for Reiki, feeling that perhaps energy work might reveal the cause of this pain in a way that other more traditional modalities had not. I gave Reiki energy to her foot, of course; but her body's messages surfaced when I had my hands over her heart Chakra. With my hands resting on her sternum, feeling it rise and fall with each breath, I asked her about any issues related to her heart that were emerging for her. She took a deep breath, let her mind and body search a bit, and then she said, "Sometimes I feel like a pushover with certain people. Like at work. Or with friends. The main issue is that I have trouble putting my foot down."

At that moment I felt goose bumps rise on my arms and wondered if my client had truly heard her own words. I echoed her last statement in the form of a question: "So you have trouble putting your foot down?" She looked at me, surprised at hearing her own statement reflected back to her.

"Yes, yes. I do. It hurts to put my foot down. It *literally* hurts to put my foot down!" This moment reinforced what I had been noticing for many years: if we truly listen, we have the ability to find insight and meaning in our very own bodies. And not only did the session give my client some insight into the emotional side of her physical pain, but she became much more aware of how her body could serve as a sort of metaphor for her life. She left the session with a bit of a skip in her step.

When working with my clients, I was keenly aware of the importance of looking to the body for guidance. I frequently worked with my clients on the emotional and psychological side that accompanied their physical discomfort. Interestingly, I noticed a particular focus in my clients, too, to question why a certain part of their body was so persistently causing them pain. Through massage therapy, energy work, coaching, and writing and art exercises, I worked with my clients to better understand their *whole* being in relation to their pain. *Body Cards* was born out of this rich and revealing work with my clients and my desire to share my approach with others who wish to explore the body's wisdom. My divination deck aims to empower people to become active in their own healing process.

While my bodywork experiences have greatly influenced my process of creating *Body Cards*, so have my experiences as a writer and artist. I have been exploring the metaphors of the body for quite some time, from my graduate school days of writing "poetry of the body" to my fascination with the human form in my art to my anatomy and physiology studies as a massage practitioner. I believe wholeheartedly that artistic expression expands our understanding of our body *and* mind and that is one reason why I chose to contribute both my words and my art to *Body Cards*. The book and deck of cards work together, deepening the metaphor of each card, for the words and images are intimately connected.

About the Chakras

The word "Chakra" means "wheel" in Sanskrit. A Chakra is an energy center and there are seven major Chakras in the body—from the base of the body (or "root") to the top of the head ("the crown"). Each Chakra corresponds with a color and an element, as well as meanings and associations on the physical, emotional, mental, and spiritual levels. You will notice that each part of the body in this deck corresponds with a Chakra, and often, the meaning of the cards is influenced by Chakra wisdom, as opening our energy centers helps us shift, change, and heal.

About the Art

Each body card image is a mixed media art piece I have created to symbolically represent the energy, essence, and deeper meaning of each part of the body used in the deck. Each art piece has a title and is meant to engage your imagination as you meditate on the meaning of the cards and includes the colors and vibrational energies of each of the Chakras. You'll notice that my art is symbolic and narrative, as opposed to representational or literal. Each art piece tells a story, sometimes even about my own life. Birds and other animals appear in my art as well. While this deck is indeed about the human body, it is also about the human body *embodied*—with life force, with spirit. Birds, in particular, represent the human spirit for me. When you see a bird on a card, pay special attention to the ways in which you might elevate your physical experience to a lighter, more spiritual one. We are human beings, but we are also human animals. Just as you take note of birds in the cards, pay attention to the other animals—dogs, cats, elephants, frogs—who may give you even more insight about your questions and quandaries.

You'll also notice stars, bursts, and other patterns, which often highlight the area of the body the card is exploring. We know that the parts of our body must work together and are integrated, interconnected, and intricately related to one another. A body part, such as the calcaneus bone or sternum, does not function in isolation. As such, you will rarely see a "disembodied" body part in the images of this deck. Instead, you will see the meaning and spiritual energy of each card symbolically relayed through color, texture, pattern, image, word, and story. Allow my art pieces on these cards to take your reading to a deeper level with your own personal growth process and allow the artistic elements of the cards to spark your imagination.

HOW TO USE THE BODY CARDS

Drawing upon the anatomy and physiology of the human body, this book explores each card in detail, illuminating characteristics that we may find in ourselves (or wish for ourselves), such as the cornea's clarity, the heart's influence, and the cerebrum's balance. The theme for each part of the body is derived from its specific location, function, unique attributes, and associated Chakra. Not only will you learn a bit more about the human body through *Body Cards*, but you will gain insight into the physical, emotional, mental, and spiritual aspects of your life.

Body Cards not only includes deep questions, insights, and suggestions related to each body part, but also a set of specific exercises enabling you to engage in your body's wisdom on a dynamic level. I provide creativity, movement, sensory, and personal growth exercises aimed at helping you to integrate the wisdom of each Chakra into your daily life. The exercises are a key component to actualizing the guidance of the cards and in transforming the way we understand our body's ability to heal.

Relating to the Cards

I like to think of this deck as a companion on your body-wise journey. The cards are meant to provide insight—a new perspective, an enlightening realization, a confirmation of something you already know deep down, and inspiration for living a creative healing life. They are perfect for daily use to help guide you—and to provide some clarity about how you might deal with any number of aspects of your life.

Selecting the Cards

In a perfect world we would sit with *Body Cards* in a quiet, clutter-free, candle-lit room when we feel calm and centered. While creating a sacred space for your card reading experience is beneficial, it's not always practical. Sometimes we're rushing off to work or an appointment and we don't have the time to find our inner Zen. *Body Cards* can be read "on the run." For a quick read, take a deep breath, set an intention, shuffle the cards, choose a card, look up the card in the book, skim the entry, including the art meditation, and then go to the "try this" section. Perhaps the suggested action from the "try this" section will support the energy of the card before you leave for your day. This exercise might be as simple as wearing a blue scarf, thumping your sternum, or massaging your ears. If you have the time and space to explore your card reading more fully, light some candles and take some time to do one of the writing, art, or meditative exercises.

Card Readings

I've created the following card readings that work well with *Body Cards*, though feel free to use spreads you use for Tarot decks or other divination/wisdom cards.

The Present Moment Spread

This spread is about right now, this very moment.

You + one card = insight

For this reading, center yourself, even if briefly, and draw one card from the deck for some power-packed guidance. Allow your body to respond to the card first, before your mind gets involved.

- What do you notice?
- What resonates on a cellular level about the meaning of the card?

Keep this card in mind as you maneuver through the intricacies of your day and pay attention to how your thinking, feeling, and actions change as a result of holding the meaning of this card in your awareness.

Letting Go Spread

1. The issue. This first card reflects an issue that relates to letting go. What in your life is waiting to be released? What is ready to shed its skin so you can move forward, move on, lift up?

2. What's holding you back? The second card reveals what issues might be holding you back in your process of letting go. For instance, if I drew the cerebrum card, I might think about whether my lack of balance or equilibrium is contributing to my stasis.

3. What will help you move forward? The third card in the spread gives you insight about what actions you might take, including addressing your own thoughts or feelings, in order to let go what no longer serves you.

Transformation Spread

1. Dreaming. Every transformational process begins with a seed, a tiny inkling of an idea or feeling. This first card represents an aspect of your developing dream, hope, or vision for yourself and your life.

2. Incubating. The second card reveals what related to your dream must incubate and mature in its own time. This cannot be rushed.

3. Hatching. We often think of hatching as a beginning, and it is to a certain extent. Hatching in the Transformation Spread is about what strength or resilience you need to step into this new place in your life. What does it take to crack the egg?

4. Fluttering. Ah, to move! The fourth card indicates what small movements or steps you should take as you get your bearings and test out your wings. What will help support you as you maneuver in this new phase?

5. Flying. The fifth and final card in this spread is the culmination of your transformation: your flight! This card shows you what blessings and challenges are in store for you in this new place, new incarnation, or new dream.

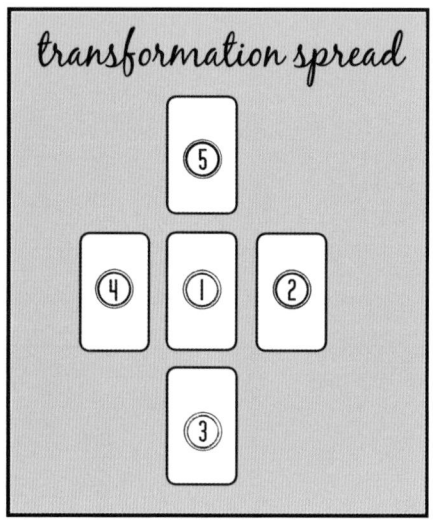

Chakra Spread

Divide the cards up into their seven Chakra categories and then draw one card from each of the Chakras. Place them in a line in front of you from the first Chakra up to the seventh at the top. (See the Contents listing for the cards by Chakra.) This reading will give you insight into the issues, gifts, and challenges of each of your energy centers.

Here is a guiding question to consider for each of the Chakras:

1. First Chakra: How might I feel more grounded in the physical world?

2. Second Chakra: How might I harness my creativity and manifest something in the world?

3. Third Chakra: What is the nature of my personal power, and how shall I use it?

4. Fourth Chakra: How do I experience deep love for others and myself?
5. Fifth Chakra: How can I speak my truth and honor my unique voice?
6. Sixth Chakra: How can I tap into my inner knowing?
7. Seventh Chakra: What is my relationship to the rest of the universe?

Interpreting the Cards

Allow the meaning of the cards to develop like a Polaroid for you. If a thought, feeling, image, or sensation about your own life strikes you right away, follow that. If you're not quite sure how a particular card or reading relates to you or your current issues, allow the cards to live with you for a day or a week and try some of the cards' exercises.

Rest assured that there is no "right way" to interpret the cards. Allow your mind, heart, body, and spirit guide in you in understanding or uncovering of what you already know. I am a firm believer in our ability to know ourselves and what is right for us. With guidance from the cards, tap into that place inside you that *already* knows. You do know what is best for you. Let your own wisdom unfold as the cards give you a little nudge.

THE BODY CARDS

AMYGDALA
Peace

Art Title: *Princely Peace*

Art Meditation: Just like the man's inner peace reaches the bird above him, allow the peace from within your mind to emanate outward, reaching others, the planet, and even the stars.

Location: The amygdala is a group of nuclei located deep in the brain in the temporal lobe.

Function: As part of the limbic system, the amygdala is involved in emotions and decision-making and is linked to our pleasure and fight-or-flight responses.

Unique Fact: When the amygdala is not functioning well, we may experience depression, PTSD, anxiety, phobias, and aggressive behaviors.

Associated Chakra: Crown (Seventh Chakra)

One of the functions of the amygdala is to help us process emotions, particularly related to fear, aggression, and anger, but also to pleasure, affection, and love. These little organs of the brain react so quickly to emotionally charged events in our lives as a way to protect us from danger and harm. Because one of the main roles of the amygdala has to do with self-preservation, it can sometimes cause us to over-react and have a fight-or-flight response, when no such response is needed. How can we cultivate peace of mind if our amygdala is so used to triggering a stress response? And on a larger scale, how can we cultivate peace in the world through our own acts of calming our lightning-fast reactionary responses?

If the amygdala has arrived in your reading, pay close attention to your relationship with inner peace. Is inner peace a feeling you recognize easily? If not, what would it take for you to recognize this feeling more often? How can you communicate to your body that not only are you safe, but you are indeed a vessel for love and peace? The message of the amygdala card is this: when you cultivate peace within yourself, you radiate that message of peace to the rest of the world. How can you harness the past pain and struggle in your life for your own serenity, but also for the good of humankind? The more you can learn to differentiate your stress responses, the more you will be able to emanate goodwill, empathy, and love to those in need. See your search for inner peace as not only a singular pursuit, but also one that reverberates far and wide.

Try This

Color: The color associated with the crown Chakra is magenta or white. To harness the energy of this card, and of the seventh Chakra in general, choose white or magenta in what you wear—from hats and scarves to necklaces and earrings to ties, shirts, and socks. For an even greater impact, wear these colors on your head or face.

Essential Oils: A few essential oils that help balance and open the crown Chakra are ylang ylang and rosewood. Add five to six drops of 100 percent essential oil to your bath, place a few drops of oil in a diffuser to scent your room, or keep a bottle of rosewood or ylang ylang in your pocket to smell when you'd like to feel more connected to your higher wisdom.

Activity: What does peace look like to you? Create a collage in which you explore the nature of both inner and outer peace. What images, colors, textures, and words resonate with you as you meditate on the possibilities of peace? Meditate on this collage daily as a way to re-connect with your feelings of inner harmony and your hopes for a peaceful world.

ARRECTOR PILI MUSCLES *Retreat*

Art Title: *Letting My Guard Down*

Art Meditation: As the warrior has chosen to turn her combative sword into the branch of a tree, you, too, can choose to transform your armor into something life-giving and life-affirming.

Location: These tiny muscles are attached to every hair follicle on the body.

Function: The arrector pili muscles involuntarily contract when we feel a strong emotion (such as fear), which causes each hair follicle on our body to raise, producing goose bumps; this hair-raising action helps us retain body heat.

Unique Fact: The arrector pili muscles are the smallest muscles in the human body: each muscle is microscopic in size.

Associated Chakra: Heart (Fourth Chakra)

Because they are controlled by the sympathetic nervous system, the arrector pili muscles engage during our fight-or-flight responses. When we feel threatened, for example, the heat in our body rushes to our core organs and muscles; in an attempt to preserve our body heat, the arrector pili muscles raise the hair on our skin. The heat-preserving effect of this action, however, does not affect humans as much as it does most other mammals. When an animal is threatened, his arrector pili muscles will contract, causing his fur to "puff up," creating a layer of warmth and making him look larger to the predator, as is the case with the porcupine. When a porcupine's quills raise, he looks fierce and threatening, causing his predator to back down (at least the porcupine hopes for this).

If the arrector pili card is giving you goose bumps today, this may signal a time to let your guard down. When your body is on fight-or-flight overdrive, as is the case when we experience repeated stress and anxiety, your body pays the price. You may become fatigued, develop pain in certain areas of your body, or experience mental exhaustion. If you find yourself in a lot of stressful situations these days, you may want to ask yourself why. Are you choosing these situations for some reason? Does the stress serve you in some way? You may also wish to explore any defensiveness appearing in your reactions to people and situations. What feels threatening and why? The arrector pili card asks you to retreat: lower your quills when there is no real threat. It asks you to know the difference between a true threat and daily stress. Find peace in knowing that your body will react when it absolutely needs to; if there is a real threat, your sympathetic nervous system will engage. For now, though, your quills can relax and reserve their energy. Take some deep breaths and remember that you are safe and protected.

Try This

Color: The color associated with the heart Chakra is green (or light pink). To harness the energy of this card, and of the fourth Chakra in general, choose green or light pink colors in what you wear—from scarves and necklaces to jackets, shirts, ties, and sweaters. For an even greater impact, wear green or light pink directly over your heart center.

Essential Oils: A few essential oils that help balance and open the heart Chakra are rose and lemon balm. Add five to six drops of 100 percent essential oil to your bath, place a few drops of oil in a diffuser to scent your room, or keep a bottle of lemon balm or rose in your pocket to smell when you'd like to feel more compassionate toward yourself and others.

Activity: Encourage the calm, tempered energy of your arrector pili muscles by calming your whole nervous system with some rose quartz. Rose quartz is a semi-precious stone, light pink in color, that can have a soothing effect. Place the stone on your chest or in your hand as you close your eyes and imagine the light pink radiating throughout your body, creating a tranquil energy for your whole mind-body system.

CALCANEUS
Foundation

Art Title: *Grounded Footing*

Art Meditation: Allow the steadiness and certainty of this bird-man's stance to remind you to trust your ability to ground yourself in times of need.

Location: The calcaneus, or heel bone, is situated at the back of the foot.

Function: The heel bone plays a load-bearing role in the body and is the insertion point for several important leg muscles, such as the gastronemius (calf) muscles, which attaches to the calcaneus via the Achilles tendon.

Unique Fact: The calcaneus is the largest bone in the foot.

Associated Chakra: Root (First Chakra)

On a daily basis your calcaneus takes a beating. It's a good thing that this large foot bone is strong and resilient, for it helps hold you up! Because the calcaneus is "load-bearing," it acts as one of the foundations of your body. Without it, we would sink, stumble, and topple under our own weight. The calcaneus is also a symbol of our need to feel solid, grounded, and to have clear, certain footing. We know that we're missing this foundation when we seem to have little or no time, energy, or resources to attend to our interests and creativity. When we're worried about our foundation—our basic needs being met—we may relegate our passions and interests to the "extra" category of our lives as we attend to the essentials.

If you've been feeling ungrounded, it could mean that you need some strong calcaneus medicine. When we aren't grounded, we feel wobbly, slippery, uncertain, and sometimes even scared. If some aspect of your life has felt precarious lately, how can you take a step forward anyway, feeling certain that you won't fall? What would it take for you to be and believe that you are solid and safe? The message of this card is to trust in the bedrock of your being. Feel the earth beneath your feet, your calcaneus bone braced beneath your weight, and trust that you will land safely because you are honoring your foundation.

Try This

Color: The color associated with the root Chakra is red. To harness the energy of this card, and of the first Chakra in general, choose red colors in what you wear—from socks and scarves to jewelry and hats. For an even greater impact, wear red in the lower half of your body to connect the color with the base or "root" of you.

Essential Oils: A few essential oils that help balance and open the root Chakra are cedarwood and patchouli. Add five to six drops of 100 percent essential oil to your bath, place a few drops of oil in a diffuser to scent your room, or keep a bottle of cedarwood or patchouli in your pocket to smell when you feel you'd like more grounding energy.

Activity: One way to feel more connected to our foundation is to go barefoot. Feel your feet, and in particular, your heel bone pressed against the floor. Rock back and forth from your toes to your heels, feeling the ease with which your body is able to balance you in the process. If you are able, try this barefoot experience outside on some soft grass where your skin can touch the earth directly. Notice how natural your body feels when rooted to the earth.

CENTRAL NERVOUS SYSTEM
Interconnection

Art Title: *Communing with Life*

Art Meditation: Feel the intricate interconnection between the girl and her bird friends and imagine how you may also feel the eternal connections between your whole being and the web of life.

Location: The brain and spinal cord make up the central nervous system.

Function: The nerves of the spinal cord receive signals from the body and send them to the brain for processing and responding.

Unique Fact: There are approximately one billion neurons, or nerve cells, in the spinal chord.

Associated Chakra: Crown (Seventh Chakra)

Your central nervous system is your center for receiving and processing information from your body. Think of it as the main "hub" of your body, allowing you to interact with and respond to internal and external stimuli with swiftness and ease. Imagine that your central nervous system is the trunk and branches of a tree. This tree is not only your foundation in many ways, but also your interconnection with the world. This tree in you connects you to the air that all creatures breathe in our world and to the earth itself, as you are firmly rooted in the ground. Take a deep breath in and feel how you nourish not only yourself, but everything and everyone around you. One breath is all breath. We are one.

If the central nervous system card has emerged in your reading, call upon the energy and intention of interconnection. The purpose of this card is to help call you out of your own world and to allow you to see the expansive universe in which you and your fellow plants and animals live. If you have been focusing too much on your own issues lately, perhaps it's time to step back and look through a wide-angle lens. Look far and wide, not just at what's in front of you. How are you connected to every other being on this planet? How might the decisions you make and the actions you take impact others? When we stay insulated in our own story for too long, we fail to see the greater picture. If you are currently working through an issue in your life, try changing your perspective by feeling that eternal, ever-expanding tree that is inside you. Feel your leaves against the sun and sky, feel your roots dipping into ground water, and acknowledge your higher purpose in this web of life.

Try This

Color: The color associated with the crown Chakra is magenta or white. To harness the energy of this card, and of the seventh Chakra in general, choose white or magenta in what you wear—from hats and scarves to necklaces and earrings to ties, shirts, and socks. For an even greater impact, wear these colors on your head or face.

Essential Oils: A few essential oils that help balance and open the crown Chakra are ylang ylang and rosewood. Add five to six drops of 100 percent essential oil to your bath, place a few drops of oil in a diffuser to scent your room, or keep a bottle of rosewood or ylang ylang in your pocket to smell when you'd like to feel more connected to your higher wisdom.

Activity: Tap into your experience of interconnection by considering this quotation from Rumi: "Goodbyes are only for those who love with their eyes. Because for those who love with heart and soul there is no such thing as separation." First, just let the words of Rumi enter your body like a breath. How do they feel? Do the words trigger any memories or feelings? How do you deal with loss and separation? Is there an essence of another that you carry with you even though you are apart? How do you carry this sense, this essence? Know you are safe and begin to write. Know that you can dip into the writing and back out as much as you need to.

CEREBELLUM
Grace

Art Title: *Balancing Grace*

Art Meditation: Allow the humble posture of the figure to remind you of your ability to show softness and grace—and to forgive yourself when you've been off balance.

Location: The cerebellum is a smaller region of the lower part of the brain, located near the brain stem.

Function: The main function of the cerebellum is to help with balance and coordination of the muscles of the body.

Unique Fact: The Latin translation for cerebellum is "little brain."

Associated Chakra: Crown (Seventh Chakra)

Without a well-functioning cerebellum, we would struggle with our balance and coordination. This part of the brain helps us perform voluntary actions like walking, yoga poses, or dancing. In essence, this "little brain" helps us to be active, balanced, and ultimately, graceful. Creating grace on a physical level allows us to feel nimble, poised, light-footed, or elegant. On a metaphorical level, embracing grace means to embrace beauty, love, and forgiveness. What in your life is in need of this humble cerebellum energy? What could be infused with the intention of beauty, which is at the foundation of grace?

When the cerebellum card waltzes into your reading, it's time to seek out grace. First take stock of your actions toward yourself and others. What could use some softening, some lightness, some love? We all have moments of being ungraceful with our thoughts or actions. The cerebellum card asks you to forgive yourself for the times in which you have been a little clumsy. It is human to be ungainly. It is human to blunder. Don't dwell on these past bumblings; instead, learn from them by intentionally adding grace to your repertoire. When in doubt, choose grace. Choose kindness and beauty. Choose to tread lightly and carefully. Choose to pause before speaking and to listen with your whole body. Choose the high road. When you choose grace, you open yourself up to the gifts of openness, connection, and transformation.

Try This

Color: The color associated with the crown Chakra is magenta or white. To harness the energy of this card, and of the seventh Chakra in general, choose white or magenta in what you wear—from hats and scarves to necklaces and earrings to ties, shirts, and socks. For an even greater impact, wear these colors on your head or face.

Essential Oils: A few essential oils that help balance and open the crown Chakra are ylang ylang and rosewood. Add five to six drops of 100 percent essential oil to your bath, place a few drops of oil in a diffuser to scent your room, or keep a bottle of rosewood or ylang ylang in your pocket to smell when you'd like to feel more connected to your higher wisdom.

Activity: Take an everyday activity or object and inject grace into it. Elevate this activity or thing with purpose, meaning, significance, and beauty! How might brushing your teeth, doing the dishes, buying groceries, or changing the oil in your car become mindful and enlightening?

When interacting with others, notice how adding some gentle elegance to your interactions impacts your communication. Notice, too, how you feel grace manifesting in your being.

CEREBRUM
Balance

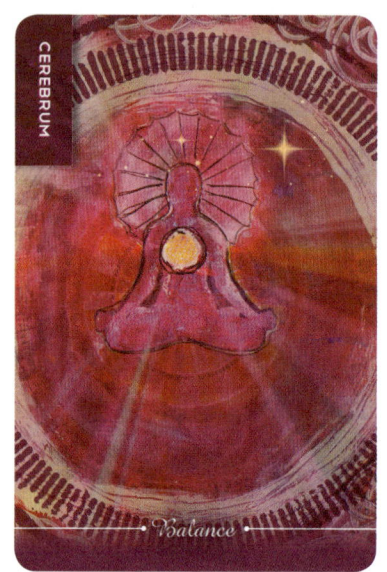

Art Title: *Radiant Equilibrium*

Art Meditation: Allow the balanced radiance of the meditating figure to give you the clarity you need to make holistic and creative decisions.

Location: The cerebrum is the largest part of the brain and is divided into four lobes: the frontal lobe, parietal lobe, occipital lobe, and temporal lobe.

Function: The cerebral cortex (the crust of the cerebrum) controls higher brain function such as thought, action, sensory perception, and emotions.

Unique Fact: The cerebrum is divided into left and right hemispheres, and its cerebral cortex comprises eighty-five percent of the brain.

Associated Chakra: Crown (Seventh Chakra)

We often use the terms "right brained" and "left brained" to describe our personality. We've deemed the right-brained person creative, intuitive, and visual and the left-brained person verbal, analytical, and sequential. The two hemispheres of the brain do in fact have different roles, which partially model this creative vs. analytical construct. But it is also true that no one is purely right- or left-brained; we are each a beautiful mixture of the two constructs. The trick is to find a balance between the two and to learn how to access the attributes of your non-dominant side. After all, you never know when your intuitive abilities might need a helping hand from your analytical side in order to solve an important problem. Or what happens when your skill at rational thought is not enough and you need take a leap of faith?

If you've drawn the cerebrum card, it may be time to gain some balance in your approach to problem solving. Whether you are dealing with a complicated mathematical problem or a dissonant conversation with your significant other, you may find that experiencing the situation through a new perspective is necessary. If your main mode for problem solving is organized and rational, but this approach gets you nowhere, try a more feeling-oriented, big-picture approach. Perhaps a little creativity is needed to alleviate a situation, or maybe your more scattered, intuitive approach could use some organized, sequential energy. By accessing both sides of your brain a "smidge" more equally, you may find that you start feeling a bit more balanced and integrated. The lesson of this card is to honor your way of being in the world, and to remember that other ways of being are inside you waiting to be tapped when you need them.

Try This

Color: The color associated with the crown Chakra is magenta or white. To harness the energy of this card, and of the seventh Chakra in general, choose white or magenta in what you wear—from hats and scarves to necklaces and earrings to ties, shirts, and socks. For an even greater impact, wear these colors on your head or face.

Essential Oils: A few essential oils that help balance and open the crown Chakra are ylang ylang and rosewood. Add five to six drops of 100 percent essential oil to your bath, place a few drops of oil in a diffuser to scent your room, or keep a bottle of rosewood or ylang ylang in your pocket to smell when you'd like to feel more connected to your higher wisdom.

Activity: Try the "breath of balance" for balancing both your brain and your life. While sitting comfortably, inhale as you raise both arms above your head, bringing your fingertips together. Then, turn your palms out and exhale as you lower your arms, bringing your fingertips toward the floor or the edge of your chair. Repeat this motion in coordination with your breath as you visualize violet (or white) light or energy flowing out from the top of your head and surrounding your whole body. This yoga breathing exercise helps balance and move energy throughout the body and helps connect the physical realm to the spiritual one.

CORNEA
Clarity

Art Title: *Seeing What Is*

Art Meditation: Just like this steadfast girl, allow your powers of observation and inner sight to burn through the busy distractions of life so you may truly see.

Location: The cornea is the transparent dome structure that lives on the front of the eye, acting as a sort of window of the eye.

Function: The function of the cornea is to protect the rest of the eye from germs, dust, and small particles; to refract light; and to focus the light into the eye.

Unique Fact: The cornea is the only part of a human body that has no blood supply, for it gets oxygen directly through the air.

Associated Chakra: Third Eye (Sixth Chakra)

The cornea helps your eyes focus so you can see clearly; it refracts the light entering your eyes and translates these light waves into your vision. When the cornea loses its focusing power, our vision becomes blurry. On a metaphorical level, our inner vision and wisdom may become obscured when we become unbalanced due to being overwhelmed. When we are overwhelmed the world does look a bit blurry, doesn't it? The myriad ideas, feelings, and complex issues we hold in our brains can cause a sense of instability and confusion. Ever try taking a photograph out the window of a moving car? That's what the psyche sees when there is just too much for us to handle.

Since clarity is the message of the cornea card, you may wish to call upon its energy to help you clear a path for more focus in your life. What, of the many things in your life, could be placed on the "do later" list so you can see more clearly the things that need your attention now? What issue in your life has felt foggy to you and how might you remove this haze so you can face it without distraction or worry? Use your powers of observation to notice where you could use some clear focus. Once you've identified what needs your attention, give yourself the time and space to allow your inner wisdom to shine brightly on your situation. Trust your intuition. Where there is light, there is vision, and where there is vision, there is clarity.

Try This

Color: The color associated with the third eye Chakra is indigo or purple. To harness the energy of this card, and of the sixth Chakra in general, choose purple colors in what you wear—from hats and scarves to necklaces and earrings to ties, shirts, and socks. For an even greater impact, wear purple colors on your head or face.

Essential Oils: A few essential oils that help balance and open the third eye Chakra are holy basil and frankincense. Add five to six drops of 100 percent essential oil to your bath, place a few drops of oil in a diffuser to scent your room, or keep a bottle of frankincense or holy basil in your pocket to smell when you'd like to feel more connected to your intuition.

Activity: To help with clarity and focus, take a walk with your camera. As you stroll through the park or around your neighborhood, notice interesting colors, shapes, and take photos of what you see. Try different angles and perspectives, too. Don't analyze your picture-taking experience too much; instead, fully experience your environment and record what's attractive to your eye. Later, view your photos and see if any themes emerge. What did you end up focusing on, and why is this significant for you?

CORPUS CALLOSUM
Communication

Art Title: *Lightning Message*

Art Meditation: Allow the powerful force of lightning to be a jolt of insight for you as you contemplate the clarity of your communication with others.

Location: The corpus callosum, a thick bundle of neural fibers, is located in the center of the brain, under the cerebrum.

Function: This band of nerves divides and connects the right and left hemispheres of the brain, allowing for communication to flow between the hemispheres.

Unique Fact: Corpus callosum means "tough body" in Latin, and it's the largest bundle of nerves in the entire nervous system.

Associated Chakra: Crown (Seventh Chakra)

The job of the corpus callosum is profound. If we didn't have this large nerve bundle, we wouldn't function properly, since the corpus callosum transfers sensory, motor, and cognitive information between the brain's hemispheres. We need the left and right sides of our brain to "talk" to each other, which is to say that one side needs to send clear nerve impulses and the other needs to be receptive to accepting and interpreting these signals. This process is much like our communication with others: if our message is not clear, then our points get lost or are received with confusion.

If the corpus callosum has appeared in your cards today, it's a time for making sure that your communication is pure in its intent, kind in its execution, and clear in its message. Consider your latest attempts at communication. Have you been impeccable with your word? Have you been kind in your delivery? Have you been the recipient of confusing information? The message of this card is to access your higher self when communicating. Speak from a place of perspective, wisdom, and higher purpose. Connect with the part of yourself that can clearly and articulately say what you mean with generosity of spirit. Now is not the time for rash words, muddled messages, and half-thoughts. Breathe love and light into your communication, and watch how smoothly it flows.

Try This

Color: The color associated with the crown Chakra is magenta or white. To harness the energy of this card, and of the seventh Chakra in general, choose white or magenta in what you wear—from hats and scarves to necklaces and earrings to ties, shirts, and socks. For an even greater impact, wear these colors on your head or face.

Essential Oils: A few essential oils that help balance and open the crown Chakra are ylang ylang and rosewood. Add five to six drops of 100 percent essential oil to your bath, place a few drops of oil in a diffuser to scent your room, or keep a bottle of rosewood or ylang ylang in your pocket to smell when you'd like to feel more connected to your higher wisdom.

Activity: To honor your corpus callosum's communicating prowess, activate and integrate both hemispheres of your brain by practicing "brain-integrating cross crawls." This is an exercise from the Brain Gym system. Slowly march in place, lifting each knee, while simultaneously tapping your opposite hand to your opposite knee. Find a nice rhythm of crossing your arms over your body to reach your opposite knee. This exercise enhances coordination and is supposed to help integrate and balance the right and left hemispheres of your brain.

DIAPHRAGM
Joy

Art Title: *Canine Companion*

Art Meditation: Allow the joy and delight expressed by this woman and her dog to breathe a new appreciation for simple gladness in your life.

Location: This dome-shaped sheath of muscle and tendon that lives in the center of the torso is attached to the lumbar vertebrae of the spine and the bottom border of the ribs and sternum.

Function: The diaphragm is the primary muscle of respiration, for it contracts (expands downward) during inspiration and relaxes during exhalation, allowing the lungs to deflate.

Unique Fact: The heart is attached to the diaphragm via its pericardium, so the heart literally rides up and down on the diaphragm as you breathe.

Associated Chakra: Solar Plexus (Third Chakra)

In the Pranayama yoga tradition, there is a breathing technique called the Breath of Joy. This breath, like a lot of conscious breathing methods, utilizes the power of the diaphragm in order to awaken and enliven your whole system. When repeating the breathing and arm movements of the Breath of Joy, oxygen floods your bloodstream, your parasympathetic nervous system is engaged, and you get a mood boost. Many of us spend much of our day doing shallow breathing (up in our chest). When using the diaphragm to breathe, we fully inhabit and revive our bodies, allowing for feelings of joy to emerge!

If the diaphragm card has arrived in your reading, the message is clear and pure: choose joy. Choosing joy does not always feel easy or natural in many circumstances. Sometimes we want to stay small and shallow, like our breath, especially when life goes awry. Are there moments, even small ones, into which you could infuse a deep, open breath of gladness? How might you remind yourself of what is going right, or going well, by breathing in feelings of gratitude and exhaling what you no longer need? By honoring your diaphragm, you are honoring your potential for wonder and joy. As you move through your day, notice when the tightness of anxiety or stress constricts your breathing, and make the choice to fill your being with life-giving breath. Surprise yourself with your innate ability to feel peace and light.

Try This

Color: The color associated with the solar plexus Chakra is yellow. To harness the energy of this card, and of the third Chakra in general, choose yellow colors in what you wear—from t-shirts and shawls to jewelry, scarves, or ties. For an even greater impact, wear yellow in your upper abdominal area at your core or center.

Essential Oils: A few essential oils that help balance and open the solar plexus Chakra are clary sage and geranium. Add five to six drops of 100 percent essential oil to your bath, place a few drops of oil in a diffuser to scent your room, or keep a bottle of geranium or clary sage in your pocket to smell when you feel you'd like more confidence.

Activity: To activate the power of your diaphragm, try some rib cage breathing. Place your hands on your ribs on the sides of your body and consciously extend your breath out horizontally. This type of breathing helps loosen the diaphragm and opens the whole rib cage / chest area that can get so tight when we are trying to protect ourselves (and more specifically, trying to protect our hearts). Imagine you are a bird extending your wings when you do this breath. Feel yourself expanding!

FINGERS
Self-assurance

Art Title: *Holding On / Letting Go*

Art Meditation: The glowing green heart of the woman hanging on so tightly to the rings asks us to contemplate who we are when we hold on to others' ideas of us and who we become when we let them go.

Location: The hand is composed of five finger bones, or digits.

Function: The fingers bend, extend, grasp, and perform a multitude of movements and tasks for us.

Unique Fact: Surprisingly, the fingers themselves contain no muscles; instead, the finger joints move because of muscles located in the palm and forearm, which connect to the fingers by strong tendons.

Associated Chakra: Heart (Fourth Chakra)

Because the fingers are controlled by the muscles in the palm and forearm, they respond much like a marionette. Our fingers don't really have minds of their own: they merely respond to the firing of muscles, which pull them to move much like the strings of a puppet. Similarly, we may find ourselves moving, acting, or being a certain way based on someone else "pulling the strings," so to speak, in our lives. When something (or someone) has such a great influence over our lives, it can feel difficult to break free and be ourselves. After all, the strings can act as a sort of support; they may hold us up if we fall. But relying on these strings for too long may in fact make you forget who exactly you are.

The fingers card reminds you to ask yourself if you are the one in control of some aspect of your life. Are there social, familial, or societal pressures that cause you to act or be in a way that is not in your nature? Is someone influencing you, and in effect making you do things that don't feel comfortable to you? The fingers are part of the heart Chakra, which has a message of self-love. You may wish to ask if you love yourself enough to cut a few of the strings that cause you to be less than yourself. It can feel challenging to cut these strings, especially if you have relied on them for a long time. Remember that the decisions you make and actions you take in your life will be much more fulfilling and meaningful when you are the one in control. Following *your* agenda, not someone else's agenda, is the message the fingers card hands you. It's time to cut some strings and trust in the wisdom of your fingers. Your self-assurance is literally in your hands.

Try This

Color: The color associated with the heart Chakra is green (or light pink). To harness the energy of this card, and of the fourth Chakra in general, choose green or light pink colors in what you wear—from scarves and necklaces to jackets, sweaters, ties, and shirts. For an even greater impact, wear green or light pink directly over your heart center.

Essential Oils: A few essential oils that help balance and open the heart Chakra are rose and lemon balm. Add five to six drops of 100 percent essential oil to your bath, place a few drops of oil in a diffuser to scent your room, or keep a bottle of lemon balm or rose in your pocket to smell when you'd like to feel more compassionate toward yourself and others.

Activity: To remind yourself to return to your heart and to trust in yourself, try this meditation with "Namaste" hands: sit comfortably with your eyes closed and shoulders relaxed. Place your hands together in a prayer-like position and press the sides of your thumbs against your sternum. This position is known as "Namaste." As you connect with your heart center, imagine green or light pink light entering your heart if you wish, for those are the colors of the heart Chakra. You may also add a heart-centered mantra as you gently breathe in and out, such as: "I trust my heart."

GLUTEUS MAXIMUS
Power

Art Title: *Seat of Potential*

Art Meditation: This woman's power is a blooming flower as she bathes in the pungent red energy of the root Chakra; take in her potential and use it as a catalyst for your own powerful flourishing.

Location: The gluteus maximus is the largest and most superficial of the three gluteal muscles that form the buttocks.

Function: The gluteus maximus helps to keep the trunk of the body erect, and extends, abducts, and laterally rotates the upper leg.

Unique Fact: The gluteus maximus is the largest muscle in the body.

Associated Chakra: Root (First Chakra)

Many of us spend most of our waking hours sitting on the largest—and one of the strongest—muscles in our entire body. There is so much power and potential in these mighty buttocks muscles; athletes rely on the gluteus maximus to help them jump higher and farther, to run faster, and to keep their body in balance while impressing us with their great feats. What great feats are we flattening, so to speak, by sitting on our seat of potential? We need not be great athletes to take advantage of the power of our backside. The power to take leaps in life, to reach the heights of our dreams, and to find personal empowerment is within our grasp. The key to tapping into this power is giving our gluteus maximus a purpose: it needs to move. *We* need to move.

If the gluteus maximus card has muscled its way into your cards, you may need to examine the untapped power that resides inside you. For certain you have this power, but you just may be sitting on it, metaphorically speaking. Perhaps this power feels a bit scary; after all, we have seen how power has been used and abused in our lives. But the pure-of-heart, well intentioned being that you are will keep this power in check. Trust in your ability to radiate your greatness with balance and compassion. Your power does not need to be forced to see the light of day; your power just *is*. It may be time to stand up and be seen. How does it feel to stand up and speak in front of a room full of people? At first you may feel a bit exposed, but the more you stand up and the more you take action, the more you will become comfortable with your own presence and power. Embrace your unique brilliance, and don't be afraid to stand in your strength.

Try This

Color: The color associated with the root Chakra is red. To harness the energy of this card, and of the first Chakra in general, choose red colors in what you wear—from skirts and scarves, jewelry and hats to ties, shirts, and socks. For an even greater impact, wear red in the lower half of your body to connect the color with the base or "root" of you.

Essential Oils: A few essential oils that help balance and open the root Chakra are cedarwood and patchouli. Add five to six drops of 100 percent essential oil to your bath, place a few drops of oil in a diffuser to scent your room, or keep a bottle of cedarwood or patchouli in your pocket to smell when you feel you'd like more grounding energy.

Activity: Dance! Yes, dance the night (or mid-morning) away with some cool tunes and your very own magnificent body. Particularly pay attention to how you shake your hips and backside. Make sure that you are giving that part of your body some ample attention and movement. Spontaneous dancing is also effective to try when you are feeling stuck. Get up out of that chair and shake your way into clarity and understanding.

HEART
Influence

Art Title: *Seeking Connection, Spreading Love*

Art Meditation: Just as this angelic woman is sharing her open and expanding heart energy with the bird, so too can you influence others with your enveloping, unconditional love.

Location: The heart muscle is located in the chest, between the lungs and behind the sternum.

Function: The function of the heart is to pump blood to the lungs and to the entire body.

Unique Fact: The heart pumps blood through approximately 60,000 miles of blood vessels in your body and can pump a person's entire blood supply in a single minute.

Associated Chakra: Heart (Fourth Chakra)

The pulse of your beating heart can be felt throughout your entire body. Just feel your inner wrist, your neck, your abdomen, your armpits, or even your feet! Blood is constantly moving through you, and your heartbeat is riding your veins and arteries, sending your unique pulse through every nook and cranny of your being. Does this pulse tend to be slow and steady or quick-paced like hummingbird wings? Whatever its rhythm, your heartbeat has a great influence on the rest of your body. Its music can make you feel deeply calm and centered or active and energized.

Just as the heartbeat can be felt throughout the human body, your words, thoughts, and actions can be felt by those around you. The rhythmic beat of the heart card signals a time of influence. It may be time to spread your abundance, your compassion, your good fortune, or your thoughtful ideas to others. Heart Chakra energy is about self-love and unconditional love. Why not offer this love to another person in need? Send the powerful beat of your influence to those close to you, or offer your deep, reverberating beat to those halfway across the world. And you may even notice that your good intentions return to you in the form of confidence, self-esteem, and self-love.

Try This

Color: The color associated with the heart Chakra is green (or light pink). To harness the energy of this card, and of the fourth Chakra in general, choose green or light pink colors in what you wear—from scarves and necklaces to jackets, sweaters, ties, and shirts. For an even greater impact, wear green or light pink directly over your heart center.

Essential Oils: A few essential oils that help balance and open the heart Chakra are rose and lemon balm. Add five to six drops of 100 percent essential oil to your bath, place a few drops of oil in a diffuser to scent your room, or keep a bottle of lemon balm or rose in your pocket to smell when you'd like to feel more compassionate toward yourself and others.

Activity: A powerful way to expand the energy of the heart is to practice the open heart gesture. An open heart gesture can come in many forms, but basically it is a stance of opening. Either sitting or standing, turn your palms up (away from your body) and extend your arms out in a relaxed way as if you are receiving a gift in each palm of your hand. In your inhalations, fill your belly and chest with what you wish to receive and then exhale what you don't need. This gesture is one of pure compassion, love, and also passivity. When we do this gesture with one another, we are saying: *I see you, I accept you, I receive you.*

KIDNEYS
Priority

Art Title: *The Fight Flies Away*

Art Meditation: As you take in the image of this kidney-turned-butterfly taking flight, reflect on how you can prioritize what flies away and what remains for your own highest good.

Location: These bean-shaped organs are located near the upper lumbar region of the spine.

Function: The kidneys remove waste products from the blood, regulate and help maintain the balance of water and electrolytes in the body, and secrete hormones that regulate the production of red blood cells.

Unique Fact: Each kidney is slightly smaller than a fist, and together, adult kidneys can filter forty-eight gallons of blood every twenty-four hours.

Associated Chakra: Sacral (Second Chakra)

The kidneys have a very important job in your body, for they help filter wastes. These two fist-sized organs know what to keep in the body and what to dispose. Now, the question is, do *you*? Imagine these fist-sized organs as two little boxing gloves, ready to fight. What is worth fighting for? Do you ever find yourself duking it out on a daily basis with little annoyances that aren't very important? When we find ourselves angry, stressed, or upset throughout the day in response to relatively small matters, we end up taxing our body-mind system. It's like giving the kidneys too many toxins to filter; when they are overworked, they don't function optimally. And neither do we.

The kidneys card signals a time for creating priorities and determining what is most important to fight for in your life. Just as the kidneys filter blood, it may be important for you to filter out the daily annoyances and irritations you experience. When we can let go of our attachment to small stresses, we build up a reserve to deal with the big stresses when they arrive. And why not spend your energy on what is truly important and worthy of your attention and your fighting spirit? What is deserving of your attention right now? A particular cause? Your health? Your relationships? The kidney card asks you to filter out the stress of a driver who cut you off, a broken dish, or an awkward moment. Let these worries move out of your system and instead focus on the "big stuff," on something you believe in.

Try This

Color: The color associated with the sacral Chakra is orange. To harness the energy of this card, and of the second Chakra in general, choose orange colors in what you wear—from pants and sweaters to jewelry and scarves. Even consider wearing orange underwear!

Essential Oils: A few essential oils that help balance and open the sacral Chakra are sandalwood and jasmine. Add five to six drops of 100 percent essential oil to your bath, place a few drops of oil in a diffuser to scent your room, or keep a bottle of jasmine or sandalwood in your pocket to smell when you feel you'd like more creative energy.

Activity: Create a mind map of important issues in your life. Start by drawing a circle in the center of a piece of paper and write an issue you'd like to explore. Then, draw lines out from the circle and create more circles with related ideas and words, until you've created a dynamic web of issues that are important to you. By creating a visual depiction of all you are considering and prioritizing, you are allowing these things to live outside you on paper, instead of in your mind.

LARYNX
Expression

Art Title: *Expressed Truth*

Art Meditation: Let the smooth currents of water, color, and air symbolize the easy flow of your own deep and creative forms of self-expression.

Location: The larynx or "voice box" is situated at the back of the tongue and extends to the tip of the trachea (windpipe).

Function: The larynx protects foreign objects from entering the trachea and allows us to produce sound.

Unique Fact: The larynx has four vocal cords: two true (active) vocal cords and two false (inactive) vocal cords.

Associated Chakra: Throat (Fifth Chakra)

Have all four of your vocal cords become inactive lately? The two cords that are supposed to be inactive are called "false" vocal cords. Have your two true vocal chords become false? In other words, are you not speaking your truth about a particular issue? Perhaps something or someone is silencing you. Or maybe you've been silencing yourself, protecting your heart by way of your throat. The problem with our own silence is that it can grow without our even noticing. As time progresses and we still haven't spoken our truth, it becomes harder and harder to release our voice. It's as if our voice atrophies from lack of use and we lose confidence in our unique expression.

If the larynx is whispering its way into your cards today, this might signal a time for raising your voice and speaking your truth. What truth are you holding deep in your throat? How long has it been there? It could be that this truth has just arrived and is waiting for the right time to come out. *Now* may be the time. If this truth has been lying in secret for a while, perhaps it's time to gently coax it out. The throat Chakra is the embodiment of voice; it is about communication, expression, and speaking with unadulterated honesty. This Chakra is also about creativity. How might your truth manifest itself once released from the depths of your throat? Will it become a conversation with a friend? A journal entry? A painting? Whatever form it takes, your voice, your truth, will have a chance to live a new life outside the confines of your silence.

Try This

Color: The color associated with the throat Chakra is blue or turquoise. To harness the energy of this card, and of the fifth Chakra in general, choose blue colors in what you wear—from hats and scarves to necklaces and jackets. For an even greater impact, wear blue directly over your throat.

Essential Oils: A few essential oils that help balance and open the throat Chakra are lavender and rosemary. Add five to six drops of 100 percent essential oil to your bath, place a few drops of oil in a diffuser to scent your room, or keep a bottle of rosemary or lavender in your pocket to smell when you'd like to feel more expressive or clear in your communication.

Activity: To honor the power and wisdom of your larynx, write about your silence and give it a voice. Where does your silence live? What happens when you know you should speak up about something and you don't? When you write about silence, you actually trick your silence into coming clean. Notice how your throat feels after you expose its censors, fears, and constrictions. Do you feel more open and clear?

LIVER
Regeneration

Art Title: *Healing Force*

Art Meditation: Sometimes healing comes lightning fast and sometimes it just takes its sweet time; either way, trust that your body knows how to renew, regenerate, and self-heal.

Location: The liver organ is located just below the diaphragm, on the right side of the upper abdomen.

Function: Among the liver's most well-known functions are the metabolism of fats, proteins, and carbohydrates; synthesis of plasma proteins; storage of glycogen, vitamins, and minerals; production of bile that helps to break down fats; and destruction of toxic substances in the blood.

Unique Fact: The liver has incredible regenerative abilities, for even with seventy-five percent tissue loss, it can regenerate into a whole liver again.

Associated Chakra: Solar Plexus (Third Chakra)

Remember the Greek myth of Prometheus? Because Prometheus stole fire from the gods and gave it to humans, he was tortured by vultures who pecked out his liver each day. But each night his liver regenerated—and the cycle continued day after day. The liver's ability to restore itself is a powerful example of our body's gift for self-healing. We cause our body distress each and every day, and yet it most often rebounds for us. We experience stress and tension, but after a good night's sleep, we often wake up calm and rejuvenated. Like

Prometheus, we begin each day renewed before life starts pecking away at us again. Remember, too, that the gods eventually freed Prometheus from this painful cycle. It may take a while, but if you believe in your body's power to heal and endure some discomfort, you, too, may be freed from your pain, just like Prometheus.

The regenerative quality of the liver is strong medicine. If the liver card is speaking to you today, it is important to listen, for the liver offers an important message about the power of our bodies to heal. Might there be something in you (on a physical or emotional level) that is trying to heal, but you are intervening too soon? Might you be pecking at your own wounds? Trust in your mind and body. Trust in yourself. There is no sense in forcing yourself to feel better. Rushing your healing is like picking at the scab before the cut has a chance to fully heal: this only causes more suffering. Remember that your very being has the ability to recreate, reproduce, and revive. If you are patient and gentle with yourself, you may discover that you heal on a much deeper level than you would have ever imagined.

Try This

Color: The color associated with the solar plexus Chakra is yellow. To harness the energy of this card, and of the third Chakra in general, choose yellow colors in what you wear—from t-shirts, ties, and shawls to jewelry and scarves. For an even greater impact, wear yellow in your upper abdominal area at your core or center.

Essential Oils: A few essential oils that help balance and open the solar plexus Chakra are clary sage and geranium. Add five to six drops of 100 percent essential oil to your bath, place a few drops of oil in a diffuser to scent your room, or keep a bottle of geranium or clary sage in your pocket to smell when you feel you'd like more confidence.

Activity: In order to tap into your innate ability to heal, try a sunflower meditation. A sunflower is emblematic of the solar plexus Chakra: its yellow color emphasizes its connection to the sun and to fire energy. Find a few quiet moments to sit and breathe into your solar plexus. Imagine that a sunflower resides right in the center of you. Its warm, glowing yellow light expands as you breathe, spreading itself throughout your whole body to every cell. Allow this beautiful sunflower yellow light to soothe you and remind you that your healing is already in process.

MASSETER
Release

Art Title: *Release the Anger*

Art Meditation: Find your own place of soft blue serenity as you turn inward like the meditating woman and let go of any tight grip you may be experiencing in your body, mind, or heart.

Location: Located in the jaw, the masseter runs vertically from the cheek bone to the mandible (lower jaw).

Function: The masseter is the major muscle of mastication, or chewing.

Unique Fact: The masseter is the strongest muscle in the body for its size.

Associated Chakra: Throat (Fifth Chakra)

Have you ever woken up from a night's sleep and discovered that your jaw is especially tight, as if you'd been grinding your teeth all night? Or what about a deep ache in your jaw during your waking hours? Many of us experience this kind of tightening in our jaw due to stress. And we often contract our masseter muscles when we are holding in strong emotions, particularly anger. It's as if we clench our jaw as an attempt to hold back our frustration or discontent. And as a result, we cause ourselves pain and we remain bottled up inside. Because the masseter muscles are strong muscles, they can often handle the tension we ask them to provide, but at what cost?

If the masseter has clenched its way into your cards today, maybe it's time you loosened your grip on some aspect of your life. What are you holding on to a bit too tightly? Is it an idea, an event, or perhaps another person? Or maybe it is your own negative self-talk that is holding you hostage. Work to unclench any anger you are carrying about yourself or others by allowing yourself to express your discontent. The more we bottle up our stress and anger, the more it tightens like a knot causing us pain. It is important to acknowledge and accept the angry thoughts and feelings we may be carrying because there is a reason for them. But we must transform these feelings so that we don't self-destruct or cause others pain in our process of anger elimination. Remember that you have the power to unlock your anger and find inner strength and peace. The answers are inside you, and with a bit of attention to releasing your jaw, you may discover that your anger turns into something surprising and beautiful.

Try This

Color: The color associated with the throat Chakra is blue or turquoise. To harness the energy of this card, and of the fifth Chakra in general, choose blue colors in what you wear—from hats and scarves, necklaces and jackets to ties, shirts, and socks. For an even greater impact, wear blue directly over your throat.

Essential Oils: A few essential oils that help balance and open the throat Chakra are lavender and rosemary. Add five to six drops of 100 percent essential oil to your bath, place a few drops of oil in a diffuser to scent your room, or keep a bottle of rosemary or lavender in your pocket to smell when you'd like to feel more expressive or clear in your communication.

Activity: To help lessen the strong grip of your jaw, place the pads of your fingers on each side of your face, below your cheek bones, and make small gentle massaging circles, moving down toward your chin and then laterally toward your jaw joints.

OLFACTORY BULB
Sensitivity

Art Title: *Sensitivity is My Strength*

Art Meditation: The smiling boy is here to remind you of how your sensitivity can bring you pain and sorrow, but also the greatest and most profound joy.

Location: The olfactory bulb is located in the frontal brain and is part of the limbic system.

Function: This neural "bulb" receives signals from olfactory (smell) receptors in the nasal cavity and sends this information to the olfactory cortex and other areas.

Unique Fact: Smell is often considered the most sensitive of the senses, most strongly linked to emotions and memory.

Associated Chakra: Third Eye (Sixth Chakra)

Your nose, and more specifically, the smelling system of your nose, your olfactory bulb, is so sensitive that with the tiniest sniff, you may experience a flood of emotions and memories you thought had long faded. Our sense of smell is so perceptive that we are transported to our childhoods with the smell of certain foods and we know almost instantly when an aroma delights or repels us. This ability to sensitively sense the world has enabled us not only to survive, but also to thrive as human beings. Our sense of smell might not be as keen as other mammals', but it's strong nonetheless, and it's our metaphorical gateway to compassionate, connected living.

If you sniffed out the olfactory bulb card today, it's a message to honor your sensitivity. When we feel and sense deeply, we may experience feeling overwhelmed and vulnerable, but we also experience our innate gift for being empathetic, sentient beings. Sensitivity is our birthright. Without it, we would have perished as a species. We have relied on our senses, like smell, for physical survival, but also for emotional connection and resiliency. If you have ever been labeled "too sensitive" in your life, you were in effect being told not to feel deeply. It's time to reclaim your keen receptivity and experience it as both vulnerable *and* powerful. Your ability to tap into your deep well of emotions enables you to experience the world fully, connect with others profoundly, and know yourself intimately. Never give that up. If you have ever been labeled "insensitive," perhaps it's also time to reclaim your receptive abilities. Empathy toward others breeds empathy toward ourselves. Reclaim your sensitivity and feel it as a source of strength.

Try This

Color: The color associated with the third eye Chakra is indigo or purple. To harness the energy of this card, and of the sixth Chakra in general, choose purple colors in what you wear—from hats and scarves to necklaces and earrings to ties, shirts, and socks. For an even greater impact, wear purple colors on your head or face.

Essential Oils: A few essential oils that help balance and open the third eye Chakra are holy basil and frankincense. Add five to six drops of 100 percent essential oil to your bath, place a few drops of oil in a diffuser to scent your room, or keep a bottle of frankincense or holy basil in your pocket to smell when you'd like to feel more connected to your intuition.

Activity: What does your sensitivity look like? Using colors—paints, crayons, or colored pencils—create a visual depiction of your sensitivity. If you want a bit more structure, get a mandala coloring book and color in the designs. Use your intuition to create a color palette that you feel represents your receptive being. After you are done, what do you notice? Do certain colors predominate? What colors most represent your sensitive self?

PANCREAS
Authenticity

Art Title: *My Own Desires Begin to Sprout*

Art Meditation: Follow the energy of the emerging figure as she grows like a seed into her authentic self, expressing her true desires and emotions.

Location: The pancreas is located across the back of the abdomen and behind the stomach.

Function: The pancreas secretes two important hormones—glucagon and insulin—which control the level of sugar in the blood.

Unique Fact: Because of its ability to keep a reserve of enzymes, the pancreas will not fail until more than ninety-five percent of its function is lost.

Associated Chakra: Solar Plexus (Third Chakra)

When the pancreas is under-producing insulin—as is the case with diabetes—the sugar levels in the blood can become dangerously high. When this happens, many health complications may arise. Monitoring how much sugar we consume is key in helping our pancreas run optimally. Similarly, monitoring how much "sweetness" we project to others is key in helping us lead balanced, authentic lives. When we give too much, say "yes" too much, and project an "everything is okay" message when it is not, we risk losing a sense of our own needs and desires.

If you find that the pancreas has sweet-talked its way into your cards today, you may wish to examine your relationship with "sweetness." Are you holding in your stress or pain and pretending your world is as sweet as maple syrup? Might you be creating too much sweetness to your detriment? Are you noticing that you are saying, "Everything is great!" and yet it's not really true? Or in another manifestation, are you being too accommodating to others, while not attending to your own needs and desires? Being liked by others can be an intoxicating feeling, one that propels us to put on a "nice face," even though we may be hurting inside. The pancreas card asks us to remember that we need to balance our sweetness. The key to this balance is in honoring your authentic feelings while being mindful of your desire to please. Remember that compassion and kindness are different from selflessness and sweetness. The message in this card is to honor yourself and others by being true to who you really are.

Try This

Color: The color associated with the solar plexus Chakra is yellow. To harness the energy of this card, and of the third Chakra in general, choose yellow colors in what you wear—from t-shirts, ties, shirts, and shawls to jewelry and scarves. For an even greater impact, wear yellow in your upper abdominal area at your core or center.

Essential Oils: A few essential oils that help balance and open the solar plexus Chakra are clary sage and geranium. Add five to six drops of 100 percent essential oil to your bath, place a few drops of oil in a diffuser to scent your room, or keep a bottle of geranium or clary sage in your pocket to smell when you feel you'd like more confidence.

Activity: For one day, try answering the question, "How are you?" truthfully. Be kind in your response, but be honest. Be honest with yourself first and then decide what fairly honest response feels best to share with others. What does it feel like to share honestly? What sorts of reactions do you receive?

PATELLA
Stability

Art Title: *Unwavering Stance*

Art Meditation: Harness the solid, stable energy of the man as he confidently greets a new day, the sun rising up before him.

Location: The patella, or kneecap, is a flat, circular-triangular bone that sits in the front of the knee-joint.

Function: The patella's job is to protect the tibia bone (in the lower leg) and the femur bone, or thighbone, and it plays an important role in bending and extending the knee.

Unique Fact: Babies are born without bony patellas, for their patellas are made of cartilage.

Associated Chakra: Root (First Chakra)

Stability is something that many of us yearn to feel. We want to feel secure and safe, knowing that we have everything accounted for and that much in our lives is under our control. We often learn that we don't have total control over many things in our lives, and yet, we still strive for that feeling of stability. While the patella bone's physical purpose is for structural stability and integrity, on a metaphorical level, it represents the constancy and dependability for which we all yearn. Think of the things in your life that you can count on. The patella epitomizes the steady certainties of life.

If you've drawn the patella card, now is the time to differentiate what you do have control over and what you don't. What in your life feels secure and stable without much effort on your part? What, on the other hand, feels insecure and wavering? Knowing that we can't always experience stability in all aspects of our lives, what do you have control over that may make you feel more secure? The knee cap protects the tibia and femur bones quite naturally. What do you naturally, or easily, have control over in your life? Start there. Consider how you can empower yourself to be a stabilizing force in your own life. What if your conscious decisions and acts on behalf of your own well being were able to boost your resolve so that you felt more safe, solid, and confident? Feel the earth's solid energy radiate up into your legs. Tap into the stability of your knees and believe in your ability to not only keep yourself from buckling over, but also in your power to thrive.

Try This

Color: The color associated with the root Chakra is red. To harness the energy of this card, and of the first Chakra in general, choose red colors in what you wear—from skirts and shirts to scarves and ties, jewelry, and hats. For an even greater impact, wear red in the lower half of your body to connect the color with the base or "root" of you.

Essential Oils: A few essential oils that help balance and open the root Chakra are cedarwood and patchouli. Add five to six drops of 100 percent essential oil to your bath, place a few drops of oil in a diffuser to scent your room, or keep a bottle of cedarwood or patchouli in your pocket to smell when you feel you'd like more grounding energy.

Activity: Divide a sheet of paper in half and on one side make a list of things in your life you feel you can control. On the other side, list things that you feel have no control over. Now freewrite about each list in your journal. What happens as you write about the things you feel you can't control? Can you come to peace with them?

PINEAL GLAND
Intuition

Art Title: *Goddess of Insight*

Art Meditation: Notice the imagery and symbols around this woman, including her vibrant third eye, connecting her (and you) to the power of intuition.

Location: The pineal gland is located in the center of the brain.

Function: This small, pine cone-shaped endocrine gland produces melatonin, a hormone that helps to regulate the sleep-wake cycle.

Unique Fact: Greek philosopher Descartes called the pineal gland the "Seat of the Soul."

Associated Chakra: Third Eye (Sixth Chakra)

The Sixth Chakra is sometimes called the "pineal eye" or "pineal Chakra," for some believe that the pineal gland is connected to supernatural abilities, intuition, telepathy, and inner wisdom. And because this tiny gland has the important job of helping to regulate our sleep-wake cycle, you might say that it is also a sort of gateway to our dream life. When our body experiences darkness, the pineal is signaled to produce melatonin for us, which helps us to sleep. And for many of us, our sleep is filled with vivid dreams, inner visions, and poignant insights.

If the pineal gland has appeared in your cards today, you may wish to explore any messages you receive in both your waking and sleeping life. Pay attention to reoccurring symbols, images, words, or feelings that come to you. If it helps, keep a notebook near your bed to record your dreams. Are there common themes or symbols in your dreams that may be of significance? And in your waking life, notice interesting repetitions and connections. Trust in your hunches and leave no synchronicity unexamined. For whatever reason, you are called now to let your intuition guide you. Let the "pineal eye" take you inside yourself and beyond yourself. What messages are you receiving—and more importantly, why are you receiving them?

Try This

Color: The color associated with the third eye Chakra is indigo or purple. To harness the energy of this card, and of the sixth Chakra in general, choose purple colors in what you wear—from hats and scarves to necklaces and earrings to ties, shirts, and socks. For an even greater impact, wear purple colors on your head or face.

Essential Oils: A few essential oils that help balance and open the third eye Chakra are holy basil and frankincense. Add five to six drops of 100 percent essential oil to your bath, place a few drops of oil in a diffuser to scent your room, or keep a bottle of frankincense or holy basil in your pocket to smell when you'd like to feel more connected to your intuition.

Activity: To help open the intuitive gifts of your third eye, try this *Om* meditation. Sit comfortably on the floor or in a chair. Bring your arms into prayer position at your third eye, so your thumbs are pressed against your nose and forehead. Chant the sound "om" (the "*om* sound actually has four parts to it: "*ah-oh-mmmmm*" + silence). No need to be perfect with this. Create an "om" sound that feels right to you. Focus on the sound and vibration of the sound you are making and imagine indigo light connecting you to your higher self. This exercise helps clear the mind, promotes grounding while clearing the upper Chakras, and energizes the pineal gland.

PITUITARY GLAND
Delegation

Art Title: *Relinquishing the Burden*

Art Meditation: This woman presenting a package asks you to consider what you can release that will help lighten the load for your own journey.

Location: The pituitary gland is located at the base of the brain.

Function: The hormones of the pituitary gland control the secretion of most glands in the body and is often called the "master gland."

Unique Fact: It's often considered to be the most protected gland in the body because it's cushioned on all sides by bone tissue.

Associated Chakra: Third Eye (Sixth Chakra)

The pituitary gland has a very important job: to delegate. If the pituitary doesn't ask the other glands in the body to secrete their hormones, these other glands won't know to perform their all-important actions. For example, without the pituitary gland knocking on the door of the luteinizing hormone, a woman would not ovulate. Without the nudges of the pituitary, our thyroid gland wouldn't know to secrete its hormones for mood balancing. And the pituitary gland can't secrete these specific hormones on its own. It must communicate its needs to the other glands, just as you might communicate your needs to your family, friends, or community.

The lesson of the pituitary card is all about taking a burden off your shoulders by asking others for help. Do you ever find yourself attending to everyone's needs but your own? Or perhaps in your current situation you are finding it difficult to carry the load by yourself. Whether this feeling of burden comes from obligations at work, at home, or with other responsibilities in your life, the pituitary card signals a time for asking for help. And you may wish to explore why it is you have this load. Is it unavoidable? Are you afraid to ask for help? Or perhaps you enjoy taking control, but this time you're in over your head. Whatever the reason, remember that delegating and asking for help is not a sign of weakness, but a great strength. When you empower others to help you, you may end up releasing the power that your particular responsibility has over you—and you may discover that you connect with others in profound and significant ways.

Try This

Color: The color associated with the third eye Chakra is indigo or purple. To harness the energy of this card, and of the sixth Chakra in general, choose purple colors in what you wear—from hats and scarves to necklaces and earrings to ties, shirts, and socks. For an even greater impact, wear purple colors on your head or face.

Essential Oils: A few essential oils that help balance and open the third eye Chakra are holy basil and frankincense. Add five to six drops of 100 percent essential oil to your bath, place a few drops of oil in a diffuser to scent your room, or keep a bottle of frankincense or holy basil in your pocket to smell when you'd like to feel more connected to your intuition.

Activity: Divide a piece of paper in half either by drawing a line or folding it. On one side write down ten things for which you want help. Don't censor or judge yourself; just write down what occurs to you. On the opposite side of the page, list ten people or resources that you feel might help you with your tasks. You now have a list of possibilities. It's time to call on one of these possibilities for assistance.

QUADRICEPS
Stamina

Art Title: *Powerhouse Elephant*

Art Meditation: The strong and resilient elephant is asking that you reflect on your staying power and your ability to be patient with the journey, no matter how heavy, long, or arduous.

Location: The quadriceps or "quad" muscles are located at the front of the thighbone.

Function: The quads help us keep an upright posture, straighten the leg, and stabilize the knee.

Unique Fact: The quadriceps muscles are considered to be one of the strongest muscle groups in the human body.

Associated Chakra: Root (First Chakra)

The quadriceps muscles help us move through the world. We rely on them to help us walk, climb, squat, jump, and run. We utilize their stabilizing powers when we stand. We feel them ache when we've overused them. These muscles remind us of our innate strength and our ability to endure—even when we're tired, even when we're unsure. We often forget to acknowledge all that these muscles do for us in our daily lives. The simple act of our walking down stairs, for example, depends on the muscular gifts of the quads or we'd tumble over. Day after day, we rely on this powerhouse group of muscles for athletic feats, moderate activities, and mundane movements. When was the last time you acknowledged your quads and thanked them for enabling you to both weather and revel in your life?

When the quadriceps muscles bound their way into your cards, this signals a time to focus on your stamina. Whether mental or physical in nature, your ability to endure requires your focus and patience. Now is the time to gather up every bit of persistence, strength, and courage you have and attend to an aspect of your life that needs the energy of one more "push" to the proverbial finish line. Perhaps you need to focus on a small problem or task that you have been avoiding or have let go dormant. Maybe you have a big project or life issue that needs even more of your attention. The quadriceps card signals a time for honoring and believing in your inner strength and stamina so you can come to a sense of completion with something important in your life. The main message of this card is "don't give up" prematurely. The other message of the quadriceps is an important one and it is this: trust in your body to know when you are done and then make the choice to stop. Don't let your exhaustion cause you to involuntarily end your process. Instead, notice when your fortitude is fraught, gracefully bring down the curtain, and give gratitude to yourself for your tenacity and courage.

Try This

Color: The color associated with the root Chakra is red. To harness the energy of this card, and of the first Chakra in general, choose red colors in what you wear—from socks, shirts, and scarves, to jewelry and hats. For an even greater impact, wear red in the lower half of your body to connect the color with the base or "root" of you.

Essential Oils: A few essential oils that help balance and open the root Chakra are cedarwood and patchouli. Add five to six drops of 100 percent essential oil to your bath, place a few drops of oil in a diffuser to scent your room, or keep a bottle of cedarwood or patchouli in your pocket to smell when you feel you'd like more grounding energy.

Activity: To connect you with your quads and to remind you of your stamina, find a moment to do a wall sit. Find a bare wall, and with your back flat against the wall, squat down so that your thighs are parallel to the floor, hold yourself there and breathe. Feel how your quad muscles tremble just a bit as you experience the strength and stamina of the base of your body.

SACRUM
Rebirth

Art Title: *Trusting the Holy Bone*

Art Meditation: A rebirth can happen at any time and the woman in her symbolic womb is asking you to trust the process, no matter how scary or confusing it may seem.

Location: Often referred to as the "tail bone," the sacrum is located at the base of the spine, made of approximately five fused vertebrae, which form the back wall of the pelvis.

Function: The sacrum joins the top part of the pelvis to form the sacroiliac joint on both sides of the lower back, allowing the trunk of our body to bend, twist, and turn.

Unique Fact: The name "sacrum" comes from the Latin *sacer*, a translation of the Greek word *hieron*, which means "sacred or strong bone."

Associated Chakra: Sacral (Second Chakra)

What makes the sacrum so sacred? Across many cultures and throughout time, people have viewed the sacrum as a "holy bone." In some cultures, an animal's sacrum was offered as part of animal sacrifices. And as it so happens, the sacrum is one of the last bones of the body to decompose; because of the sacrum's long life and resiliency, some cultures believed that the sacrum allowed people to return from the dead. It's inspiring to imagine a sacrum bone as a seed, regrowing the pelvis, adding muscles and ligaments, and eventually forming the whole human body! What is sacred in *you* that could be resurrected from an idle or dormant place?

If the sacrum is unearthed from your cards today, it may be time to resurrect some part of yourself that you've buried. Perhaps there is a part of you—your playful side, your creative side, or your spiritual side—that used to see the light of day, but out of fear or boredom or self-consciousness, you threw a heap of dirt on it. It could be that this aspect of yourself is just what you need right now in your current situation. The second Chakra, also called the sacral or reproductive Chakra, is all about the creative life force. It could be, too, that some creative action, expression, or problem-solving is needed now. It may be the perfect time for whatever it is that you've kept deep inside to emerge after a long hibernation sleep. Celebrate its return and give it a new, splendid life.

Try This

Color: The color associated with the sacral Chakra is orange. To harness the energy of this card, and of the second Chakra in general, choose orange colors in what you wear—from pants and sweaters to jewelry and scarves. Even consider wearing orange underwear!

Essential Oils: A few essential oils that help balance and open the sacral Chakra are sandalwood and jasmine. Add five to six drops of 100 percent essential oil to your bath, place a few drops of oil in a diffuser to scent your room, or keep a bottle of jasmine or sandalwood in your pocket to smell when you feel you'd like more creative energy.

Activity: Reconnect with your creative life force by finger painting. It's time for a rebirth of your creativity and there's no better way than getting a little messy in the process. Get some paper and a variety of tempera paints and go to town. Don't worry so much about *what* you are creating as much as *that* you are creating. Allow this childlike act of creativity to spark whatever inspiration you are wanting to rekindle in your life.

SCALENE MUSCLES
Honesty

Art Title: *Carrying the Nest*

Art Meditation: Allow the weight of the nest on this woman's head to remind you that much of what you are carrying might be contributing to your stress—and that you can, with self-honesty, let this stress fly away.

Location: There are three scalene muscles on each side of the neck, running vertically from the cervical vertebrae to the first and second ribs.

Function: The scalenes lift the upper ribs during normal inhalation and help in flexing and rotating the head to each side.

Unique Fact: The scalene muscles are named after the scalene triangle from geometry: these muscles, along with the clavicle bone, create an uneven triangle shape in the neck.

Associated Chakra: Throat (Fifth Chakra)

When the scalene muscles tighten, an interconnected series of symptoms can occur. For example, when the scalenes constrict, sometimes they bind the brachial plexus, the nerve bundle that runs from the neck down through the arm, ending at the fingers. When this constriction happens, people may experience pain, numbness, or tingling down their arm. When we hike up our shoulders and ribs for significant periods of time—as is the case when we are stressed—we also cause stress to our scalenes. And if our scalenes are constricted, this also means that we may be experiencing short and shallow breath. Lack of deep breath can contribute to headaches and other pain in the body. Stress and lack of full breath may cause a whole series of physical and emotional tensions reacting much like the domino effect. What is at the core of your stress? What stress in your life has this kind of lasting power and influence? What do you find triggers your stress response?

The scalene muscles card asks you to honestly look at the root cause of any stress you are experiencing and to understand how this stress contributes to any pain—physical or emotional—that you feel as a result. Something as simple as hiking up your shoulders can contribute to a whole series of discomforts. Sometimes the root cause of our stress can feel elusive to us. It's time to dig deeply to find the action, belief, circumstance, habit, or area of tension that is causing your system to weaken. Is there a limiting belief you hold that is causing a ricochet of low self-esteem or lack of confidence? Is there a particular unhealthy habit you have that causes a cascade of other poor habits? The scalene card signals a time of being honest with yourself about what is causing you stress. Trace back your steps or draw yourself a map if you need to; the point is to resolve and soothe the root of the problem so your whole system will benefit. Remember that correcting just one side-effect of the problem is only a Band-Aid solution. Locate the source and empower yourself to make positive and lasting change.

Try This

Color: The color associated with the throat Chakra is blue or turquoise. To harness the energy of this card, and of the fifth Chakra in general, choose blue colors in what you wear—from hats and scarves to necklaces and jackets. For an even greater impact, wear blue directly over your throat.

Essential Oils: A few essential oils that help balance and open the throat Chakra are lavender and rosemary. Add five to six drops of 100 percent essential oil to your bath, place a few drops of oil in a diffuser to scent your room, or keep a bottle of rosemary or lavender in your pocket to smell when you'd like to feel more expressive or clear in your communication.

Activity: Draw your pain. You need not consider yourself an artist by any means. The purpose is to express your pain—whether physical or emotional in nature—in visual form. Be messy and scribble if you feel so called. Get underneath your pain by making it tangible on the page, and begin to see how it might transform when you take an honest look at it.

SKIN
Renewal

Art Title: *Stitching My Life Back Together*

Art Meditation: Just as the bird-woman is acknowledging the skin she is in right now and is creating her own future, consider how you can embrace the present moment with all your heart.

Location: As the largest organ of the body, the skin covers your entire body.

Function: The skin insulates and protects the body from the elements, regulates body temperature, and senses touch, pressure, cold, heat, and pain.

Unique Fact: In one year, approximately nine pounds of skin is shed from the human body.

Associated Chakra: Heart (Fourth Chakra)

The skin has an astounding ability to renew itself. Every day, we shed a layer of dead skin cells, and every month we develop an entirely new layer of skin. This process of renewal happens in our very own body whether we notice it or not. We shed our skin, like our past, and become new again to face the present moment. While remembering and learning from the past can be helpful (and even therapeutic), it can also cause us to remain stuck in a previous reality. The past can also serve to haunt us, reminding us of mistakes or pain that is no longer part of who we are now. And fixating on the past may cause us to be oblivious to our current situation.

If the skin has sloughed its way into your cards today, it may signal a time of shedding your attachment to the past. If you are noticing yourself holding on to the past in your current situation, it may be a time to examine the reasons why. Is the past more comfortable? More pleasant? Do you connect more clearly to the person you were five, ten, or twenty years ago? Or does the person you were in the past constantly remind you of who you don't wish to be? The skin card asks you to look at the beautiful human being you are *right now*. The past can certainly inform your decisions now, but don't let it govern them. Remember that just like your skin, you are resilient and protected this very moment. Your past does not define you. *Today* does. And just like the shedding power of the skin, you will be different tomorrow . . . and the day after that. It's time to accept that you are a dynamic, ever-changing human being with the power to be whoever you wish to be.

Try This

Color: The color associated with the heart Chakra is green (or light pink). To harness the energy of this card, and of the fourth Chakra in general, choose green or light pink colors in what you wear—from scarves and necklaces to jackets, sweaters, ties, and shirts. For an even greater impact, wear green or light pink directly over your heart center.

Essential Oils: A few essential oils that help balance and open the heart Chakra are rose and lemon balm. Add five to six drops of 100 percent essential oil to your bath, place a few drops of oil in a diffuser to scent your room, or keep a bottle of lemon balm or rose in your pocket to smell when you'd like to feel more compassionate toward yourself and others.

Activity: Honor your skin by nourishing it. After a shower or bath, mix a few drops of rose oil in an organic carrier oil such as coconut oil or jojoba oil and massage it into your skin. Allow your skin to soak in the moisture as well as the healing attributes of the rose essential oil.

SMALL INTESTINE
Patience

Art Title: *The Art of Waiting*

Art Meditation: As the bird learns to patiently sit on her nest, ask yourself how can you learn to trust your patient process of creative unfolding.

Location: The small intestine begins at the stomach and winds its way through our lower abdomen, finally connecting to the large intestine, or colon.

Function: This important organ digests our food and absorbs the food's nutrients into the blood stream.

Unique Fact: The small intestine in an adult human is approximately twenty-one feet long.

Associated Chakra: Sacral (Second Chakra)

The process of digestion is a long, winding journey. Because the majority of digestion and absorption of nutrients happens in the small intestine, this famously long organ plays a very important role in the health of your body. When we eat foods that do not nourish us, our digestional organs tell us with their grumbles, pains, and other uncomfortable manifestations. Similarly, when we find some idea disagreeable, we feel this negative energy in our body. But when we resonate with an idea or action, our body knows it and gives us positive signs. That's why it is important to remain clear about what we resonate with and find nourishing to us and not let others interfere with our process of digesting our ideas. We don't want to let another's less-than-positive reaction stifle our digestive process.

The twists and turns of the small intestine card are a reminder to allow something to fully digest before letting it see the light of day. This can be difficult, especially when we love our ideas and want to share the enthusiasm we feel. The small intestine is part of the second Chakra, a Chakra all about creative manifestation. Do you have an idea, a project, a plan, or a piece of writing or art that is moving through you? This card signals a time of slow digestion. Allow yourself the time to live with your ideas and let them digest slowly and easily. Often, when we release our precious ideas too soon, the positive energy we have for them dissipates before our eyes. Another person's luke-warm reaction may dampen our enthusiasm, or our inner critic suddenly emerges when we vocalize our dreams and visions. Practice patience and trust that your creative juices will provide the right amount of time for you to digest your creation. You will know when you are ready to share your work and ideas; you will feel it deep in your gut.

Try This

Color: The color associated with the sacral Chakra is orange. To harness the energy of this card, and of the second Chakra in general, choose orange colors in what you wear—from pants and sweaters to jewelry and scarves. Even consider wearing orange underwear!

Essential Oils: A few essential oils that help balance and open the sacral Chakra are sandalwood and jasmine. Add five to six drops of 100 percent essential oil to your bath, place a few drops of oil in a diffuser to scent your room, or keep a bottle of jasmine or sandalwood in your pocket to smell when you feel you'd like more creative energy.

Activity: When you find yourself frustrated by your own impatience, take a moment to center yourself in the present moment through your breath. Breathe down into your belly, allowing it to gently expand. Conscious breathing not only quiets the mind, but it refocuses you. It allows you to become clear about your next steps without the feeling of urgency or impatience. Let your body show you how to let your life unfold naturally and in its own time.

SOLEUS MUSCLES
Action

Art Title: *Burst of Action*

Art Meditation: Allow the spirited and vibrant energy of the butterfly-winged woman to propel you into glorious, discerning action!

Location: As one of the muscles of each calf, the soleus muscle sits under the gastronemius (calf) muscles, which are more superficial.

Function: The soleus aids in balance and walking, and along with the other calf muscles, pumps venous blood back to the heart from the lower extremities.

Unique Fact: Due to its fish-like shape, the word "soleus" comes from the word for "sole fish."

Associated Chakra: Root (First Chakra)

The soleus muscles are often called "The Second Hearts" for they return blood from the lower extremities to the heart through their pumping action. That's why exercise is so important for circulating blood throughout your body. These "little hearts" require action in order to function properly; without movement, we can become stagnant in our heart. All our heart's desires, like our all-important blood, could be pooling at our feet!

If you find that the soleus muscle is pumping its way into your cards, perhaps it's time to feed your heart's desire through action. Have you been envisioning something for quite a while, yet are resistant or scared to take action? It's important to "feel right" before we take action, but maybe you're ready to take the leap right now. What's holding you back? Move your way into manifesting something important to you. Go ahead: tell someone you love them; take that new job; enter that juried art show; sign up for that marathon. The soleus card signals a time of doing. Ask your heart what it desires and then allow yourself the chance to move your way into manifesting your dreams.

Try This

Color: The color associated with the root Chakra is red. To harness the energy of this card, and of the first Chakra in general, choose red colors in what you wear—from socks, shirts, and scarves to jewelry, jackets, and hats. For an even greater impact, wear red in the lower half of your body to connect the color with the base or "root" of you.

Essential Oils: A few essential oils that help balance and open the root Chakra are cedarwood and patchouli. Add five to six drops of 100 percent essential oil to your bath, place a few drops of oil in a diffuser to scent your room, or keep a bottle of cedarwood or patchouli in your pocket to smell when you feel you'd like more grounding energy.

Activity: Connect with the wisdom of your soleus muscle by jumping! The next time you are feeling caught in stagnation mode, jump! Use a mini trampoline or bounce on your regular, old living-room floor. Move your body and this will move your mind. Don't try to figure out what's next. Don't think. Jump. The answers will follow through your actions.

SPLEEN
Willpower

Art Title: *The Prayer of Will*

Art Meditation: Look deep within yourself, like the girl in prayer, to find your motivation, your inspiration, and your willpower.

Location: The spleen is an organ located in the upper left portion of the abdomen, to the left of the stomach and under the rib cage.

Function: In addition to filtering and purifying blood, the spleen is also part of the immune system and helps fight unwanted microbes in the blood.

Unique Fact: In Chinese medicine, emotional states associated with an unbalanced spleen are worrying, obsessing over things, and overthinking.

Associated Chakra: Solar Plexus (Third Chakra)

The purpose of the spleen is to filter and purify your blood, and as a result, your body's immune system stays strong. The spleen helps you fight infections, enabling you to not only stay healthy, but to thrive. In the realm of Chinese medicine, the emotional energy of the spleen is about overthinking and worry. When the spleen's willpower is disrupted, we may experience mental exhaustion and fearful, obsessive thoughts. Worrying without action is particularly harmful, for doing so keeps us stuck in a stew of distress. We don't want to be marinating in our worries. Instead, we want to move with and through our concerning thoughts. In all, we need to take action.

The spleen in a card reading represents willpower, and more specifically, your commitment to stop any obsessive worry cycles you may experience. Your willpower in this regard comes from your intentional and persistent acts on your own behalf. You have the power to calm your worries. This ability resides inside you, whether you feel its presence or not. Whatever issue is plaguing you at this time can be managed when you access the wisdom of the spleen. Just as the spleen filters the blood, you need to filter your destructive thoughts and worries. Ghandi once said, "Strength does not come from physical capacity. It comes from an indomitable will." Acknowledge your worries, but know that they cannot overpower you if you don't let them. Take intentional action, even tiny baby steps, toward addressing your worries. Allow the worries to live outside of you—through your actions—so they don't pollute your system from the inside. Trust in your commitment and drive. Trust in your willpower. You can do this.

Try This

Color: The color associated with the solar plexus Chakra is yellow. To harness the energy of this card, and of the third Chakra in general, choose yellow colors in what you wear—from t-shirts and shawls to jewelry, scarves, and ties. For an even greater impact, wear yellow in your upper abdominal area at your core or center.

Essential Oils: A few essential oils that help balance and open the solar plexus Chakra are clary sage and geranium. Add five to six drops of 100 percent essential oil to your bath, place a few drops of oil in a diffuser to scent your room, or keep a bottle of geranium or clary sage in your pocket to smell when you feel you'd like more confidence.

Activity: The words "I am" are potent words. They come from our center and they connect with our sense of confidence and willpower. The solar plexus is, energetically, where individuality and sense of self reside. For this writing exercise, start every sentence with "I am" until you can't any longer—until your "I ams" have runneth over and you are full. See if you can push yourself just a bit more when you get to the point when you feel you are done. I am…I am…I am….

STERNUM
Protection

Art Title: *The Bird Within the Bird*

Art Meditation: The heart-protected bird asks you to tap into your authentic feelings, to express them, and in the process, to know you are safe.

Location: The sternum bone is located in the center of the chest and articulates with the clavicle bones and first seven pairs of ribs.

Function: The sternum, also known as the breastbone, serves to protect the heart, lungs, and main blood vessels from physical damage.

Unique Fact: During open-heart surgery, the sternum is cut open to gain access to the heart.

Associated Chakra: Heart (Fourth Chakra)

The strong sternum bone provides a layer of protection for those all-important ingredients of your body: your lungs and heart and major blood vessels. On an emotional level, the breastbone is often a place where we place our hand when we are moved or in some way affected emotionally. It is here on our chest where we can feel our own (or another's) heartbeat and the rhythm of our breathing. The sternum bone can feel like a powerful center for connecting with our own feelings or the feelings of others, for it is here where we often feel love and affection for another. And during a grief process, our heart Chakra often emits a tremendous amount of energy as we feel our losses deeply.

The sternum card appears to remind you that your heart is always protected—that you can feel deeply and you will not crumble into a million pieces. If you have been resisting your body's call to feel love, grief, joy, or sadness, this may be time to take the risk and let the emotions come. When we hold our emotions tightly in our chest, we trap them there to live constricted, unexpressed lives. When we hold in our feelings, we may feel tightness in our chest and lack of full breath. It can feel like a risk to feel deeply, but the message of the sternum is that of safety and protection. And while showing your emotions to another can feel exposing and intense, this sharing can also be deeply satisfying and freeing. What feelings are pulsing in your chest at your sternum, waiting to be released? Place your hand on your breastbone, feeling the powerful pulse of your own heart, and ask yourself what emotions are ready to become known. Face your feelings with openness and compassion, knowing you are safe and protected.

Try This

Color: The color associated with the heart Chakra is green (or light pink). To harness the energy of this card, and of the fourth Chakra in general, choose green or light pink colors in what you wear—from scarves and necklaces to jackets, sweaters, ties, and shirts. For an even greater impact, wear green or light pink directly over your heart center.

Essential Oils: A few essential oils that help balance and open the heart Chakra are rose and lemon balm. Add five to six drops of 100 percent essential oil to your bath, place a few drops of oil in a diffuser to scent your room, or keep a bottle of lemon balm or rose in your pocket to smell when you'd like to feel more compassionate toward yourself and others.

Activity: Connect with the energy and wisdom of your sternum by doing the thymus tap. Gently tap your sternum with the pads of your right hand in a waltz beat (*one-two-three*, pause, *one-two-three*). This beat increases the production of T-cells, which in turn boosts your immunity and energy, relieves stress, and increases your resolve and resiliency. Also notice the strength of your sternum as you feel and listen to the thump-thump that echoes in your chest.

STIRRUP BONE
Listening

Art Title: *The Art of Vibration*

Art Meditation: Allow the ripples of sound to emanate as you allow beauty—like birds, water, and flowers—to enter your soundscape.

Location: The stirrup bone is located in the middle ear, a narrow air-filled space between the outer and inner ear.

Function: The stirrup is a U-shaped bone that sends sound vibrations to the cochlea in the inner ear.

Unique Fact: The smallest bone in the human body is the stirrup bone and it stays the same size from birth until death.

Associated Chakra: Third Eye (Sixth Chakra)

Sometimes the tiniest of things can impact the way you experience the world. The stirrup bone, smaller than a grain of rice and situated in a tiny space in your ear, enables you to hear. Such a useful little bone! And yet, listening is not just a physiological act, it is also a deeply emotional one. Our little stirrup bone can be vibrating away, but we may not be hearing a thing. Have you ever taken stock to notice when you "tune out" and stop listening? Are there certain topics of conversation that repel you? What about particular sounds or tones of voice? For many of us, particular childhood (or even adult) memories come to mind when we contemplate when and why we stop listening. Perhaps someone was cruel or mean with their voice. It makes sense that in order to protect ourselves, we shut down and plugged our ears. Perhaps there is part of you that is still that child, waiting for the bad sounds to stop.

If the stirrup bone is appearing to you, this may be a sign to take your fingers out of your ears. Is there something important you are not hearing because you are afraid to listen? Is there a particular truth that you're avoiding? And how well are you listening to yourself and your inner wisdom these days? Remember that when we tune out the dissonant sounds of the world, we often tune out the beautiful sounds as well. Listening is an art form, and when you can embrace this receptive art truly and fully, you may find that even the dissonant sounds have purpose. You may also discover that you begin to attract insightful voices, beautiful melodies, and other open and compassionate ears, ready to listen to *you*.

Try This

Color: The color associated with the third eye Chakra is indigo or purple. To harness the energy of this card, and of the sixth Chakra in general, choose purple colors in what you wear—from hats and scarves to necklaces and earrings to ties, shirts, and socks. For an even greater impact, wear purple colors on your head or face.

Essential Oils: A few essential oils that help balance and open the third eye Chakra are holy basil and frankincense. Add five to six drops of 100 percent essential oil to your bath, place a few drops of oil in a diffuser to scent your room, or keep a bottle of frankincense or holy basil in your pocket to smell when you'd like to feel more connected to your intuition.

Activity: There are literally hundreds of acupuncture points in your ears. When you perform a simple massage for your ears, you are able to access all of the points. And self-massage of the ears also promotes better listening skills, which honors the power of your stirrup bone!

STOMACH
Affirmation

Art Title: Authentic Affirmations

Art Meditation: Allow the solar glow emanating from the woman's center to shine brightly, but gently, on the positive affirmations you are creating.

Location: The stomach organ is located in the upper left quadrant of the abdomen, connected to the throat by the esophagus, while the lower end empties its contents into the small intestine.

Function: The stomach is involved in the second phase of digestion, preparing your food for further digestion and absorption by the small intestine.

Unique Fact: The hydrochloric acid present in the human stomach is potent enough to dissolve a nail.

Associated Chakra: Solar Plexus (Third Chakra)

The digestive process would not be possible without the strong gastric juices of the stomach. It is amazing to think that we would burn our skin if we touched those acids. The protective lining of the stomach is tough enough to endure these acids so we don't burn ourselves from the inside. Gastric juices need to be powerful to do their job, but they need not sting us. Think of the acid in your stomach as the critic inside us, which can help us to be discerning and to digest and process important issues in our lives. This inner critic can help us live authentically and impeccably, but it can also stifle us and burn away at our self-confidence and inner resolve. That's why it's important to keep this inner critic in check and to learn when to use its influence to your advantage and when to keep the sting of this inner voice at bay.

The message of the stomach card can be summed up in the following phrase: "Don't let your own acids burn you up." It may be time to examine when this inner critic most surfaces in your life. Is it at work? When you are creating art? When with your family? What triggers this cranky, critical voice to surface? Are there times when someone or something unnerves you enough to break your self-confidence? The stomach card asks you to challenge the inner voice that tells you that you are not good enough. Build your own protective lining and replace negative self-talk with specific and meaningful affirmations. The key here is specificity, for the more specific you are with your positive statements the more clarity you bring to your own sense of self. When you tell yourself, "I am a good person" (which you should!), try taking your self-talk to a bit deeper and more specific place, such as "I bring empathy and honesty to my relationships." The inner critic has a much more difficult time dissolving such thoughtful and specific statements. Allow your positive statements to soothe you and find peace in your ability to control when and how your inner voice speaks to you.

Try This

Color: The color associated with the solar plexus Chakra is yellow. To harness the energy of this card, and of the third Chakra in general, choose yellow colors in what you wear—from t-shirts and shawls to jewelry, scarves and ties. For an even greater impact, wear yellow in your upper abdominal area at your core or center.

Essential Oils: A few essential oils that help balance and open the solar plexus Chakra are clary sage and geranium. Add five to six drops of 100 percent essential oil to your bath, place a few drops of oil in a diffuser to scent your room, or keep a bottle of geranium or clary sage in your pocket to smell when you feel you'd like more confidence.

Activity: Because the stomach card is about how to deal with the proverbial acids inside you, this writing prompt is all about fire energy, which happens to be the element associated with the solar plexus Chakra. How do you experience fire energy in your life? When do you feel fiery? Are you comfortable with the blazing, crackling, hot, passionate fiery aspects of yourself? Light a candle before you sit down to write. Watch the flickering flame, smell the wax, feel the tiny bit of heat it emits. Now write from your inner pilot light—that fire inside your gut. What fuels your fire? What extinguishes it? Feel your solar plexus with your hand. What's right there, in your center, waiting to be expressed?

TEETH
Commitment

Art Title: *Enameled Wisdom*

Art Meditation: The girl's bright, certain smile signifies a time for you to feel your commitment to your words and deeds.

Location: The teeth are held in place by periodontal ligaments, which attach each tooth to a jaw bone, and gums.

Function: The primary functions of teeth are for chewing, and together with the tongue, speech.

Unique Fact: Made of mineral calcium phosphate, the enamel of teeth is the hardest tissue in the entire body.

Associated Chakra: Throat (Fifth Chakra)

Chewing is an act of strength and conviction. When we use our strong, enameled teeth to chew, we are taking clear action and then processing the result of that action (digestion). When we have problems with our teeth, eating becomes difficult, and we may need to use soft or liquid food to nourish us because we are not able to carry out the pulverizing task of mastication. When our teeth are healthy and strong, we can tackle even the most unyielding carrot. When optimal, our teeth remind us of our inner strength. They symbolize our ability to take on challenging tasks, to execute with confidence, and ultimately, to speak our truth and to commit to it through our actions.

When the teeth come chomping into your reading, you are being asked to look at what you say and what you do. Are you speaking your truth, but then avoiding taking action? Do you find yourself feeling vehemently about something only to slink away from the actions that might align with your values? Teeth remind us to act with clear intention and to manifest our convictions with confidence. Don't stop short. Your voice is needed. Your perspective is important. Your principles need a place to live. Commit to walking your talk. Remember not to bite off more than you can chew, but make sure you are finding ways to honor the energy of your teeth by acting on your word. Your level of commitment can be measured by how you follow through with what you say and with what you do.

Try This

Color: The color associated with the throat Chakra is blue or turquoise. To harness the energy of this card, and of the fifth Chakra in general, choose blue colors in what you wear—from hats and scarves to necklaces and jackets. For an even greater impact, wear blue directly over your throat.

Essential Oils: A few essential oils that help balance and open the throat Chakra are lavender and rosemary. Add five to six drops of 100 percent essential oil to your bath, place a few drops of oil in a diffuser to scent your room, or keep a bottle of rosemary or lavender in your pocket to smell when you'd like to feel more expressive or clear in your communication.

Activity: Write from the perspective of your committed teeth as if they had their own voice. What has been locked down by your teeth, waiting to be released? What is unsaid? What do your teeth say that you talk about, but haven't yet done? Take the perspective of your teeth and allow your imagination to flow.

THYROID GLAND
Transformation

Art Title: *Metamorphosis*

Art Meditation: Allow the blue butterfly of transformation to inspire your own expansion and personal growth.

Location: The thyroid gland is located in the throat, in front of the trachea, and below the larynx.

Function: The thyroid produces hormones that regulate metabolic rate and bone metabolism.

Unique Fact: The thyroid gland has a butterfly shape.

Associated Chakra: Throat (Fifth Chakra)

One of the main functions of your thyroid gland is to metabolize the nutrients in your body into energy. This transformation allows your body to function properly. Who knew that this little gland, weighing less than an ounce and shaped like a butterfly, would play such an important role! Physiologically, your body's cells survive and thrive by converting, changing, exchanging, and metabolizing. Your physical body is in fact in a constant state of metamorphosis. With your body's cells on a regular rotation of death, rebirth, and transformation, this butterfly inside you represents the ever-present possibility for metamorphosis and transformation. Change is your birthright. You experience perpetual evolution whether you realize it or not, and it is impossible to be stagnant. Your body, via the thyroid gland, is giving you a message about your innate ability to move gracefully with the energy of change.

When the thyroid gland flutters into your reading, it's time to meditate on your relationship to change. Do you welcome change in your life? Or does change cause you to recoil back into the cocoon? The message of the thyroid gland is clear: choose transformation. A very important aspect of the throat Chakra is choice. You can choose to stay inside the safety of the cocoon and you can also choose to fly. What will your choice be? There is at least some part of you ready and waiting to experience transformation. What is holding you back? The thyroid gland card asks you to consider taking action on behalf of that butterfly inside you. Honor your body's ability to shift and change by doing the same for some aspect of your life. Now is the time to reveal to the world your beauty, your gifts, your strength, and your truth—in all, to reveal your remarkable butterfly wings.

Try This

Color: The color associated with the throat Chakra is blue or turquoise. To harness the energy of this card, and of the fifth Chakra in general, choose blue colors in what you wear—from hats and scarves to necklaces and jackets. For an even greater impact, wear blue directly over your throat.

Essential Oils: A few essential oils that help balance and open the throat Chakra are lavender and rosemary. Add five to six drops of 100 percent essential oil to your bath, place a few drops of oil in a diffuser to scent your room, or keep a bottle of rosemary or lavender in your pocket to smell when you'd like to feel more expressive or clear in your communication.

Activity: To encourage your process of transformation, loosen the muscles in your neck. The neck can become very tight when we feel resistance within ourselves. Often, when we are holding our voice back, our neck muscles tighten. Place your hands on the back of your neck and make small gentle circles on the posterior neck muscles. Make sure to massage all the way up to the base of your head where the neck muscles attach to your skull. Remember to breathe gently and allow your neck and throat to soften.

UMBILICUS
Connection

Art Title: *Nourishing Art*

Art Meditation: The bird-artist is at work, nurturing her artistic life, asking you to awaken your own creativity as you connect with your feminine life force energy.

Location: The umbilicus, or belly button, rests in the abdomen.

Function: There is no formal function of the umbilicus since it is the scar that remains after the umbilical cord has been removed at birth.

Unique Fact: This scar contains a plethora of bacteria unique to each person.

Associated Chakra: Sacral (Second Chakra)

The umbilicus, or belly button, is one of our most visible signs of our connection to creative life force. Our navel scars are reminders of our path to existence, of the nourishment we received in order to grow, and of our connection to maternal energy and the Great Mother Earth. The belly button represents our eternal connection to feminine creativity, regardless of our gender, and this little button pouch in the body unites us all. Regardless of whether we identify our belly buttons as "innies," "outies," or invisible, we each were connected to our mothers by the umbilical cord and we each had this physical connection severed in order to live separately, wholly ourselves. We have all taken this journey from the amniotic womb into this world.

When the umbilicus appears in your cards, it's time to reconnect yourself with your natural ability to create. After all, you created this very life you are living. Even if you don't consider yourself "creative," your umbilicus tells you otherwise. The metaphor of the umbilicus asks you to reawaken the creative feminine force that brought you here and to resuscitate dormant creativity. How can you use the power of this scar to help you harness your imagination, vision, and ingenuity? What small act can you take that will reconnect you with your innate ability to produce beauty in whatever form? How can you connect to others through your act of creating, and even more significantly, how can you deeply connect with yourself?

Try This

Color: The color associated with the sacral Chakra is orange. To harness the energy of this card, and of the second Chakra in general, choose orange colors in what you wear—from pants and sweaters to jewelry and scarves. Even consider wearing orange underwear!

Essential Oils: A few essential oils that help balance and open the sacral Chakra are sandalwood and jasmine. Add five to six drops of 100 percent essential oil to your bath, place a few drops of oil in a diffuser to scent your room, or keep a bottle of jasmine or sandalwood in your pocket to smell when you feel you'd like more creative energy.

Activity: Reawaken your feminine creativity by creating a goddess collage. Using simple cut-out images and a glue stick, create a collage of the feminine force within you. Allow your intuition to guide you as you find images and put them together to create your vision goddess energy. When you are finished, place it somewhere special where you can see it daily to remind you of your connection to this part of yourself.

UTERUS
Manifestation

Art Title: *Being and Doing*

Art Meditation: Allow the woman's powerful womb-energy to reignite your commitment to your purpose, your values, and your deeds.

Location: The uterus, or womb, is an organ located in the middle abdomen and is part of the female reproductive system.

Function: The uterus nourishes a fertilized egg and is responsible for the growth of an embryo and fetus during pregnancy.

Unique Fact: During the course of a pregnancy, the uterus increases fifteen to twenty times in weight.

Associated Chakra: Sacral (Second Chakra)

Regardless of whether you use your uterus to create life or not—or whether you even have a uterus—the energy of the womb is inside everyone. All human beings can say that the uterus was once their home. And we all emerged from the uterus, one way or another, breathed in oxygen, and began the process of creating our lives. Our ability to create, generate, and manifest is innate. We thrive on being evolving, productive creatures. When we manifest our ideas, thoughts, musings, and feelings into something tangible in the world, we are honoring our process of actualization.

The message of the uterus card is manifestation. Who we become is, in large part, related to what we create. Do we create peace of mind, harmony, discernment, integrity, or justice through our actions? What do we reveal about ourselves (and *to* ourselves) when we are in alignment with our sense of purpose? If the uterus card has arrived in your reading, it's time stop thinking about what you want to manifest, and to *do* it. If you value transparency, be transparent. If honesty is important, manifest honesty. Don't wait for someone else to do it. Don't wait to feel "ready," for this feeling may never come in the way you want it to. Instead, manifest what you want to see and experience in the world. Use the life-giving power of the uterus to help you reveal your gifts in walking your talk, speaking your truth, and being the person you want to be.

Try This

Color: The color associated with the sacral Chakra is orange. To harness the energy of this card, and of the second Chakra in general, choose orange colors in what you wear—from pants and sweaters to jewelry and scarves. Even consider wearing orange underwear!

Essential Oils: A few essential oils that help balance and open the sacral Chakra are sandalwood and jasmine. Add five to six drops of 100 percent essential oil to your bath, place a few drops of oil in a diffuser to scent your room, or keep a bottle of jasmine or sandalwood in your pocket to smell when you feel you'd like more creative energy.

Activity: Start your process of manifestation by first writing down what you want to manifest. For this writing exercise, write in the first person and in the present tense. For example: "I am ready and willing to open my heart again and find love" or "My confidence feels nourishing and natural." Write as if what you want is already in your life and part of you.

BIBLIOGRAPHY

Biel, Andrew. *Trail Guide to the Body: How to Locate Muscles, Bones and More*. Boulder, CO: Andrew Biel, 1997.

Dennison, Paul E., and Gail Dennison. *Brain Gym: Simple Activities for Whole Brain Learning*. Glendale, CA: Edu-Kinesthetics, 1986.

Eden, Donna, and David Feinstein. *Energy Medicine: Balance Your Body's Energies for Optimal Health, Joy, and Vitality*. New York: Jeremy P. Tarcher/Putnam, 1998.

Lee, John H., and Ceci Kritsberg. *Writing from the Body: For Writers, Artists, and Dreamers Who Long to Free Your Voice*. New York: St. Martin's Press, 1994.

Mercier, Patricia. *Chakras: Balance Your Body's Energy for Health and Harmony*. New York: Godsfield Press, 2000.

Mercier, Patricia. *The Chakra Bible: The Definitive Guide to Working with Chakras*. New York: Sterling, 2007.

Salvo, Susan G. *Massage Therapy: Principles & Practice*. 2nd ed. Philadelphia: W.B. Saunders, 1999.

LIST OF CARDS BY CHAKRA

ROOT CHAKRA

Calcaneus: Foundation
Gluteus Maximus: Power
Patella: Stability
Quadriceps: Stamina
Soleus Muscles: Action

 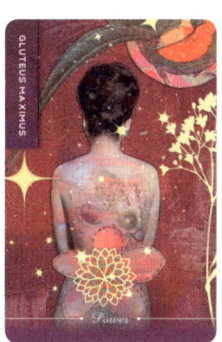 

SACRAL CHAKRA

Kidneys: Priority
Sacrum: Rebirth
Small Intestine: Patience
Umbilicus: Connection
Uterus: Manifestation

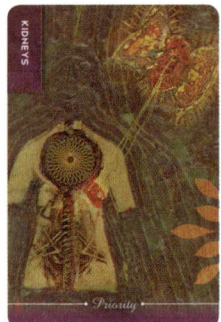  

SOLAR PLEXUS CHAKRA

Diaphragm: Joy
Liver: Regeneration
Pancreas: Authenticity
Spleen: Willpower
Stomach: Affirmation

HEART CHAKRA

Arrector Pili Muscles: Retreat
Fingers: Self-assurance
Heart: Influence
Skin: Renewal
Sternum: Protection

THROAT CHAKRA

Larynx: Expression
Masseter: Release
Scalene Muscles: Honesty
Teeth: Commitment
Thyroid Gland: Transformation

THIRD EYE CHAKRA

Cornea: Clarity
Olfactory Bulb: Sensitivity
Pineal Gland: Intuition
Pituitary Gland: Delegation
Stirrup Bone: Listening

CROWN CHAKRA

Amygdala: Peace
Central Nervous System: Interconnection
Cerebellum: Grace
Cerebrum: Balance
Corpus Callosum: Communication

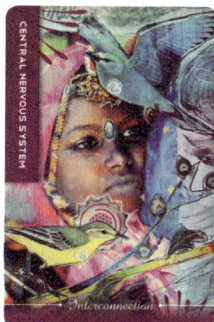
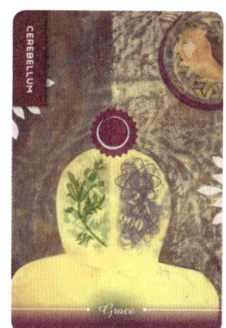
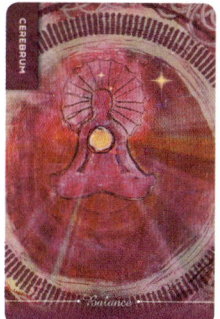